The Ultimate Customer Support Executive
Unleash the Power of Your Customer

The Ultimate Customer Support Executive

Unleash the Power of Your Customer

Phil Verghis

SILICON PRESS
www.silicon-press.com

Silicon Press
Summit, NJ 07901
USA

First Edition
Printing 9 8 7 6 5 4 3 2 1   Year 09 08 07 06

Library of Congress Cataloging-in-Publication Data

Verghis, Philip, 1966-
    The Ultimate Customer Support Executive: Unleash the Power of the
Customer / by Phil Verghis
    p. cm.
    Includes bibliographical references and index.
    ISBN 0-929306-34-1 (alk. paper)
    1. Customer services--Management--Handbooks, manuals, etc.
    2. Executives--Handbooks, manuals, etc.
    I. Title.

HF5415.5.V49 2005
658.8'12--dc22

                    2005002319

*To all those who fight to unleash
the power of the customer within
their organizations.*

More power to you!

Contents

Preface

Getting and keeping profitable customers for life is critical in this hyper-competitive world. But this is just wishful thinking without the successful convergence of people, processes and technology. Working together, these ingredients can unleash the power of the customer to propel your company to new levels of success.

Why is it that most people in support try to get out as quickly as possible? Why is it that the people who know the most about customers and can make or break the reputation of a company – indeed make or break the brand itself – are routinely ignored and do not have any influence in the corporation?

A big part of this is *our* problem – those of us in customer support. Externally, we are often viewed by customers as the 'helpless customer support team', some combination of friendly but clueless script-followers. Internally, we are often seen as the group that takes grief from our customers, but cannot articulate that grief in a way that's meaningful to the rest of the company. We are not perceived as powerful enough to hold anyone's feet to the fire, so we're not taken seriously.

I've seen over and over again how individual departments in an organization can optimize their customer support, but if it is not examined from the customer's perspective, they end up with a sub-optimal experience.

This book covers both internal support and external support, which are historically separate worlds. While much of this is similar, you will find the most differences in the *Process* chapter, where internal support is more likely to use common industry techniques. Although the book was written to be read sequentially, feel free to jump from chapter to chapter.

When you are finished reading the book, I hope you will participate in the support community and share your expertise with others.

As I've progressed through my career, first in support, then management and now as a consultant to organizations around the world, I've discerned some common threads in terms of what makes an Ultimate Customer Support Executive and, frankly, what does not. This book is the result of what I've learned so far on my personal journey – a journey which is by no means complete.

Acknowledgements

I'd like to thank my editor, Tom McKay of Maine Creative, and my publisher, Narain Gehani of Silicon-Press. My appreciation to all those who agreed to be interviewed and particular thanks to Joe Fleischer, Chief Technical Editor, *Call Center Magazine*, for reading and reviewing parts of the manuscript.

Also special thanks to my wife and our extended families. Thank you for all your love and support.

1 Leadership

A leader takes people where they want to go. A great leader takes people where they don't necessarily want to go, but ought to be.

— Rosalynn Carter, former First Lady of the United States

While there are a number of excellent books that talk about leadership, I'd like to concentrate on leadership from the context of a support executive.

Outstanding support executives share four traits:

- Leadership style
- Knowledge
- Expectations
- Passion

Leadership Style

Leadership style is the range of appropriate leadership techniques one might use in different situations.

Using different styles at different times and under different circumstances is not something that comes naturally to most of us — at least at work. There are three reasons for this.

First, in our business life we tend to use whatever works for us in our personal life. This is a mistake. The more senior you are, the more you are required to put organization needs first, team needs second and personal considerations third.

Most of us have a hard time separating "business" decisions from personal decisions, particularly in non-European cultures.

For example: Suppose you are someone who cares deeply about people's feelings. You may not be able to fire

1

someone, despite their demonstrated and repeated inability to do their job. Instead, you feel bad for them and keep giving them another chance. You forget that by not dealing with the situation quickly and forthrightly, you are negatively affecting other people's jobs and morale.

Second, most people use a leadership style that works for them. Typically it's how they want to be treated, and so they use almost exclusively. This wouldn't be a problem if everyone had the same style and preferred to be treated the same way. This is not the case, obviously, and can be very frustrating.

For example: Many people in customer support tend to be "relationship-based," in which interactions between people proceed on the basis of their relationship. Sales people tend to be "transaction-based" in their relationships. They are very friendly during the transaction. When the transaction is over, the relationship is effectively on hold until the next transaction.

This makes many customer support people think that sales people are insincere. But that's just because this type of behavior is different from how support people tend to interact. Recognize the difference, and get over it.

Third, if you're a top performer in support and stick around long enough, you may find yourself promoted to manager. It's one of the few ways you can be rewarded. I call this "manager as musician." You know how to play one instrument really well, so you get promoted to conductor.

Unfortunately, when you are promoted to manager, there is often no training. No one explains how to be a good manager, or what little training you do receive comes from someone who was never trained themselves. Result: You will probably pay lots of attention to those parts of the job you know well, and leave the rest to other experts in your team.

It takes skill and hard work to move to "manager as conductor," in which you know all the musical instruments pretty well – but not nearly as well as the professionals playing them.

Perhaps you were the person that everyone counted on to get things done. You might even have operated under the idea, "If it has to be done, and done right, I have to do it myself." It will be scary for you to start entrusting important projects to others.

In these cases, don't worry about the journey or even (sometimes) the results. Set clear expectations with your team, then step back and let them reach the destination in their own way. Inspect only at the appropriate milestones that you have jointly agreed to, unless they come to you for assistance or guidance before then. Resist the urge to check in on the team's progress frequently. Their job is already interrupt-driven, and they don't need you looking over their shoulders. They will not relish you scrutinizing every detail of their task (as opposed to the outcome of the task.) They will see it as a lack of trust.

You must also allow others to develop as leaders, even if it means they use techniques different from yours in order to do so.

Tip: Using different leadership styles for different situations and groups does not mean that you should be inconsistent or sway with the wind. Your core principles should never change, no matter what. Examples of core principles include your moral and ethical standards, as well as ensuring that you are always operating with integrity. These core principles should never be in doubt. Neither you nor your team should ever stray from them.

Knowledge

These days man knows the price of everything but the value of nothing.

— Oscar Wilde, Irish poet, novelist

In order to be respected by your bosses, your staff and your peers, you must have *domain knowledge*. This means you must be a master of customer support. If you are to become an Ultimate Customer Support Executive, you should know the most about the field of customer support and service in your entire organization.

In order to do this, you must keep up with the best practices for people, process and technology in your field. Stay abreast of the latest standards, become industry certified (discussed in more detail in Chapter 5, *People*) and become a thought leader (someone whom others look up to as a source of innovative and new ideas).

You must develop *people-specific knowledge*. This means you should know your team very well, no matter how many layers down the organization chart any particular team member might be. Make it a point to understand what makes them tick.

Customer support is a people-intensive business. Your individual success lies in making other members of your team successful. The sooner you understand that, the faster your career will advance.

You must also have *organization-specific knowledge*. You must know your organization's products or services very well. That sounds obvious, but most support people don't know much about their company's products or services, or where each fits into the organization's portfolio of services. Do you stumble and mumble when asked what your organization does? Do you know your company's "elevator sales pitch?"[1]

Tip: If you have a pre-sales technical team, look at their documentation and presentations for ways to explain and position your organization's products and services. For those in the non-profit world, find out what your fundraisers pitch to potential donors.

Expectations

Treat a man as he is, he will remain so. Treat a man the way he can be and ought to be, and he will become as he can be and should be.

— Johann Wolfgang von Goethe, German poet, novelist

In 1968, Harvard professor Robert Rosenthal and Leonore Jacobson, principal of a San Francisco elementary school, published a book titled *Pygmalion in the Classroom: Teacher Expectation and Pupils' Intellectual Development.* The basic premise of the book was this: When teachers expect students to do well and show intellectual growth, they do. When teachers don't have such expectations, performance and growth may be discouraged in a variety of ways.

The authors cited an experiment in one school. Teachers were led to believe that certain students were likely to show signs of an intellectual and developmental "growth spurt." In reality, the students had been chosen at random. But at the end of the year, the prophesy became self-fulfilling. The students who had been singled out showed significantly greater gains in intellectual growth than those not in the control group.

I think these findings are applicable in many areas, including customer support. Even well intentioned customer support executives assume that working in this field is merely a stepping stone to a better career in engineering or some other department. An Ultimate Customer Support Executive must embody the belief that customer support is a worthy destination in its own right, not just a stop along the way to another career.

Set high expectations, both for yourself as well as your team. These should be tough, but not impossible, to achieve. Children are good with computers (indeed with all technology) because they are not afraid to fail. Young people don't know what is "impossible," so they often accomplish it. Your team should be given the freedom to dream of what's possible – not constantly be reminded of why something is impossible.

Passion

> *I'd rather be a failure at something I love than a success at something I hate.*
>
> – George Burns, comedian

Having passion for what you do is exceptionally important, particularly when your job is stressful. Let's face it, customer support is stressful. People calling in for assistance usually aren't very happy to begin with. Passion is something you cannot fake – in life or in business. Either you love your work, or you don't. When you love what you do, it shows, and you get people's attention. When you have passion for your job, you don't mind the long hours you spend at work, and you come back home tired but thoroughly content.

Without passion, you can still be a very good support leader. But all the *great* support leaders I've met over the years have had a strong passion for what they do. Most often that passion focuses on helping other people.

Tip: Be careful of being too passionate, however. There is a fine line between being passionate and being dogmatic. You don't want people to confuse your passion with being obstinate and inflexible. Remember, your core principles are the only things that you won't be flexible on. Also, don't confuse the lack of "rah-rah" histrionics as lack of passion.

2 Who Are You?

The most pathetic person in the world is someone who has sight, but has no vision.

– Helen Keller, American author and lecturer

Most organizations have a vision statement and a mission statement. Very few people can actually remember them, and even fewer can recite them with a straight face. Both are important in their own way, but there is another statement that is perhaps most useful from a practical, day to day point of view. I call it the litmus statement. Let's review all three.

Creating a Vision Statement

A vision statement is a statement of what your organization would like to become. Keep it short and memorable. It should be a touchstone that allows your team to understand what to do when rules don't cover the situation. Sometimes customers and corporate partners will want to see it to understand what you aspire to be.

If it's too long, a vision statement can sound like a child's wish list: "I want to be a firewoman, a doctor, an astronaut and the President." When translated into organization-speak, it can read like a laundry list, a jumble of platitudes that excite no one. When I was the Manager of Technical Services at the Office of Information Technology at Duke University in North Carolina, USA, we created a vision statement for our help desk.

Our vision statement was "to create a world-class help desk that is a benchmark for other universities." This statement enabled us to compare ourselves with other university support centers around the world. One of the measures of success we set was attracting visits from other universities. After we put into practice a number of new procedures and tools, we had a number of visitors from other universities that used us as a benchmark for success. Thanks in part to our vision statement, we were named one of the best of the best help desks within the first year of our relaunch by completely revamping our people management, processes and technology, all on a relatively small budget.

Creating a Mission Statement

A mission statement describes how you will achieve your vision. This is useful mostly as an internal goal, and probably will mean nothing to the vast majority of your customers. Once again, if your mission statement is too long, it becomes meaningless.

There is at least one good use for a mission statement. If you are involved with internal support (i.e., supporting internal customers rather than external customers) or are part of a large corporation with lots of bureaucracy, a mission statement can help prevent "scope creep." This is where the agreed-to scope of a project keeps expanding incrementally. Little by little, you're doing more and more.

Scope creep typically involves adding responsibilities without a commensurate increase in resources or flexibility of schedules to make it happen. It's one of the biggest morale killers for a support staff. "They want us to do *what?* With no extra staff?" Having a mission statement helps start a meaningful dialogue to see if a new task is really within the scope of what you are supposed to do.

> *For example:* Let's say you work at a university support team. Your mission statement says that you assist faculty, staff and students. What about visitors to the University-affiliated hotel? Who takes care of the slightly inebriated guest who is trying to connect to the Internet at 2 am and work on a presentation? By looking at your mission

statement, you (and your boss) can see if this is within the scope of your mission. This does not mean blindly following procedures and refusing a guest who needs help. It means helping each customer to the best of your ability at that point, but ensuring that the process is scalable so that other guests can also be helped in the future.

Creating a Litmus Statement

You have heard a lot about vision and mission statements. But what on earth is a "litmus statement?" It's a short, one-sentence statement of what your team does that no other team does.

No other group outside your organization is going to remember your vision or mission statement. Heck, you should feel glad when your own team does. However, when things are changing very fast, there is usually confusion over who does what.

Between 1999 and 2001, for example, revenues at Akamai Technologies, a Cambridge, MA-based global distributed computing provider, grew from about $4 million to $163 million (US). During this time, the company grew from about 150 employees to roughly 1,500 employees, acquired three companies, and added new product lines very rapidly.

It was a period of frantic growth. As Akamai's Vice President of Infrastructure & Support, I promoted the use of litmus statements among my teams. They helped us remember, without any hesitation or doubt, who was responsible for what. Indeed, they helped the staff remain sane.

Examples: The Akamai Network Operations Center's litmus test described itself as "the eyes, ears and hands" of the network. Account Management "owned the *business* relationship with the customer." Customer Support "owned the *technical* relationship with the customer."

Why the distinction between the technical relationship and the business relationship with the customer? Very simple. Customer Support couldn't win the battle with the sales team over who owned the relationship – Sales did. But Customer Support did own the technical part of the relationship, which was something sales certainly didn't want to handle. This also eliminated any doubt about who had the final say over any aspect of the customer relationship – Account Management did. If decisions had to be made quickly, Customer Support knew they had to coordinate with Account Management.

Three Important Roles

An Ultimate Customer Support Executive plays three critical roles in the organization: customer champion, company champion and staff champion.

Customer Champion

You and your group are the champions for the customer within your organization. Fundamentally, this is what customer advocacy is all about. To become the Ultimate Customer Support Executive and to unleash the power of your customer, this is a prerequisite. You must become a fierce champion for the customer. You must fight to eliminate any obstacle that stands in the way of the customer getting the very best customer experience.

Remember, no matter why customers originally bought your products or services, they stay, upgrade or buy more because of quality and customer service.

To do your job properly, you must get to the root cause of each and every issue (incident) the customer has, before you consider an issue resolved. Few support people spend time looking at the root cause of an incident. Instead, they spend most of their time managing and reporting on the symptoms (which is often what incidents are) rather than the cause of the incident.

An incident, according to ITIL,[1] is "an event which is not part of the standard operation of a system that causes, or may cause, an interruption to or a reduction in the quality of service." What most people would call the root cause, ITIL calls "the problem." It's defined as "an unknown, underlying cause of one or more incidents."

Resolving an incident may keep the customer happy for now. But leaving the root cause unresolved won't keep customers from running into the same problem later. Remember, you represent the customer. So you should not allow problems to get closed until you and your support staff are completely satisfied that the root cause has been resolved, or will be in a timely manner.

How do you resolve problems that cause ongoing customer grief or internal pain? Pick up the phone, or if you can, go in person to the team that is responsible for solving the problem. Talk with the team leaders (or directly with the team if that makes sense in your organization). Invite the leaders and key influencers in the team to see firsthand what the real problem is, and how it affects your team.

In addition, your reports should mention the incident(s) and the root cause (problem), along with the work being done to resolve them. If that doesn't help expedite the resolution of a long standing problem, use reports to make your point – subtly at first, then forcefully and very publicly if needed.

One technique I have found that quickly resolves ongoing customer issues is listing problems by the internal group accountable for resolving them. Specify how long each has been open, and include them in your weekly report to management. If the delay is due to a lack of resources or some other factor, this is your chance to work with your counterpart in the team responsible for resolving the issue, and get appropriate resources allocated to solve these nagging problems.

Since you are the customer champion, you should closely analyze every interaction that your company has with a customer. Make sure each is a great experience. One often-overlooked area is billing.

If you do your job well, this may be the only contact some of your customers will have with you. Since another department (e.g., Accounts Payable) often gets the bill, be sure your contact information is correct, just in case the customer has questions about their bill. I've seen payments consistently delayed because of something as simple as that. This can affect the DSOs or "Days Sales Outstanding," a measure Wall Street uses to see how promptly people pay their financial obligations to you.

I cannot stress this point strongly enough: If you (and your team) are not champions of the customer, you have failed in your mission. Move to another job.

Company Champion

So you represent the customer to your company. But at the same time, you and your team are the champions of the company to your customers. You are the "face" of your company. That means customers will often blame you when something goes wrong – even if it is out of your control. In those situations, be careful you don't give customers the wrong impression. You don't want to appear to be taking sides against your own organization. A typical rookie[2] mistake is to say something like, "Yes, I sympathize. 'They' often push a product out before it is ready." If reading this brings a little smile to your face, if this is true in your company – make sure it stops immediately. This attitude should never be shared with customers. By all means, fix the problem – but also fix your attitude.

Remember, you and your team are representatives of your company. So the correct attitude is, *we* screwed up, and here is what *we* are going to do to make things right. It's *us*, not *them*. (Of course, if the customer has responsibilities and accountabilities towards the resolution, make sure those are also clearly spelled out too.)

Staff Champion

So you are a customer champion and a company champion. But that's not all. There will be times when customers or even your colleagues in other departments will start bashing your staff. You've seen it. Certain customers don't want to speak to a particular person because of their ethnicity or sex. You've also seen people take out their frustration and anger on your staff, since they are the most visible, and the most convenient to criticize.

It is very important that you deal with this quickly and forthrightly. You cannot allow your staff to get verbally abused without standing up for them. It's a morale killer. If you desert them when they're under fire, they will desert you, and you can expect high staff turnover. Customer support staff understand that people call to complain or because they are unhappy. What they don't understand and won't accept is their leaders allowing abusive situations to develop without sticking up for them.

Here is a pretty good test to see if you are mostly thinking as a staff champion and not as a company champion. As a team leader or a junior manager, your first loyalty is naturally slanted to your team, rather than the company. But as you move up and become a senior manager or director, your first loyalty must be to your company or institution. This means that you first determine the right thing to do from the company's perspective, and then consider how it will impact people.

> *Example:* You're a newly promoted manager, and you have been told in confidence that your closely-knit team, along with the rest of the employees in that location, are going to be laid off. Do you tell your team in advance (after swearing them to secrecy, of course)? Or do you do the right thing by the company and inform them at the proper time? If you are seriously tempted to tell the team ahead of time, then you are still thinking like a staff champion, no matter what your title is. You need to re-orient your way of thinking. You must learn to think of

the company first in order to become an Ultimate Customer Support Executive.

3 Customers

There is only one boss. The customer. And he can fire everybody in the company from the chairman on down, simply by spending his money somewhere else.

— Sam Walton, founder of Wal-Mart

Being a part of the service industry requires an enhanced understanding of your customer. After all, the customer's expectations and your behaviors greatly influence their experience with your company.

Customer Lifecycle

A business exists for one reason: to help its customers succeed. Too many organizations think only in terms of the widgets they produce or the services they offer. For example, as a purchaser of a computer, you don't use it because it has fantastic features at a reasonable cost. That may have been the reason you purchased it, but it is not the reason you use it.

Chances are you bought the computer to do work of some kind. Sure, you may also use it to play games or send email to friends and family. But if you bought a computer for work, your primary reason was because you believed it would help you succeed in accomplishing your goals. It is important to broaden your understanding of why your company is in business, to grasp why people use your company's products or services. You must have the vision to see beyond the break/fix aspects of support.

As part of a customer support team, you either provide support directly to customers, or to someone who deals directly with customers – for example, sales.

To be an Ultimate Customer Support Executive, you must look beyond what the average support person sees. You must pay careful attention to the entire customer lifecycle. This includes prospective customers, direct customers, indirect customers, delinquent and "past due" customers and former customers.

I know that most of you are thinking, "We don't have time for this! We barely have enough time to keep up with our existing customers." The truth is, the right efforts at the right times at various points in the customer lifecycle will reap significant dividends and mean less work down the line.

Prospective Customers

Prospects may have expressed an interest in your company's good or services, but have not yet become paying customers. So why bother with prospects? Because setting proper expectations is one of the key elements of a service interaction, so this is precisely the point when your influence with the prospective customer and indeed within your company should begin.

It's important to note that customer support should not be talking directly to prospective customers unless explicitly asked to by sales. Having said that, however, getting to know more about prospects *before* they become customers is a smart move. Learn why they're considering your company, and how they expect to improve their business by working with you. This will help you see things from the customer's perspective, not just a support perspective. Understanding a customer's needs and goals also eases you into your role as a customer champion.

Work with your sales department to ensure that you understand and can meet the needs of prospective customers (including a reseller's customers and international customers). Will your current service offerings meet their needs? If extra preparations are needed on your end, coordinate with engineering and other teams as necessary to ensure a flawless customer experience.

Knowing a prospect's "hot button" issues will help your support team understand the customer's business goals and why they're considering becoming a customer. Remember, the value you provide is solving the customer's problems, and understanding what they are trying to accomplish is the first step.

Important: It goes without saying that sharing confidential customer information within your company should be done with the utmost discretion. You should never ever share this type of information with people outside your company. Inform your team that any breach of confidentiality will result in immediate termination.

Setting Prospective Customer's Expectations

Take a good look at your company's pre-sales process. What are your pre-sales consultants saying about your support procedures and implementation times? Are unrealistic, "blue sky" promises being made, just to close a sale? Can you actually deliver what they're promising?

Make sure your company's sales people fully understand that they have a responsibility to ensure that any special support requirements are clearly communicated to your team, and agreed to by both sides. If you have a variety of service offerings at different price points, this is also where the upselling process begins.

Tip: There is a good reason why McDonald's asks, "Would you like fries with that?" The power of suggestion is very strong.

Let me repeat once again: Customer service should not be talking directly to prospective customers unless explicitly asked to by sales.

Direct Customers

It is critical to know your customers really well. Most of you are nodding your heads in agreement at this point. "Of course I do. Want to see a few of my detailed reports?" But I'm talking about more than the people who contact you for assistance. You should have complete mastery of that information. But what do you know about the customers who *don't* contact you? More importantly, do you know *why* they do not contact you?

When was the last time you did a service audit of all of your customers?[1] That's where you'll discover those customers who have not contacted you. Why haven't they? Is it because everything's great? Or because they find you difficult to do business with? Perhaps they no longer use your products or services. If so, you should pass that information to sales immediately.

Are they getting support formally from some other organization? Or informally, from knowledgeable internal people? In the first case you have a great opportunity to correct the situation by proving your capabilities are superior to the third party support organization. In the latter case it is quite possible that the informal support they receive is less efficient (and less accurate!) than support from your team of professionals. Both situations represent a sales opportunity. In either case, customers who are entitled to support but do not use it could be expensive to your business because of the disruption to each other's productivity as they ask other non-support professionals for help. Don't assume that a customer who doesn't contact you is a happy customer. Find out why first.

Indirect Customers

When thinking about customers, it's easy to forget about a group that often contributes a significant amount of your company's revenue: customers that come through the reseller channel. Many companies use resellers to increase their market share without increasing their direct sales force. In technical support, these "resold" customers are one of the most neglected portions of a business.

The more removed you are from directly interacting with a customer, the greater the likelihood of a customer experience that's less than ideal. An Ultimate Customer Support Executive always tries to improve the quality of customer interaction.

Indirect customer support typically involves two types of problems. The first occurs when there is a mismatch between the quality of the service the customer gets from the reseller, compared to directly from your team. In other words, the reseller's customer service is inferior to yours. If the reseller's support standards and delivery are comparable to yours, then there's no problem. Unfortunately, you most likely have no way of knowing if this is the case. In fact, most often you have no way even to see what kind of service your reseller's customers are getting.

The second type of problem happens most commonly when the product or service is complex, and good customer support requires a deep knowledge of the product or service. Due to the inherent nature of this type of support, the reseller's support team must often rely on your support team for assistance. It doesn't take long for the customer to figure this out. Soon your reseller's customers may start coming to you directly for support. But wait. Your company's financial models may assume that the resellers are delivering support (and being paid for it), when in reality, your team might be providing it at no charge. This is not a good situation from a business perspective.

A number of high-level strategies can minimize the risk with both these issues.

- *Start early.* You have the most influence during the reseller contract stage. Too often reseller support contracts are treated just like straightforward support contracts with direct customers. Instead, you must take into account the complexities of having a third party involved with the customer. Create a flowchart of the support path, and make sure it makes sense from the resold customer's point of view, and your company's financial model.

- *Build comprehensive, reseller-specific training.* Be sure to build in mandatory refresher courses so the reseller's team is always up to date on the best practices. Stagger releases so resellers have to be certified before they are allowed to sell the latest products or services. (You'd be surprised how often this is overlooked.)
- *Partner with your internal reseller sales team* to ensure that your provisioning tools are "reseller ready" from day one. Provisioning tools get customers up and running with your products or services. Tools that are "reseller ready" means the reseller can use them to setup their customers without having to involve anyone at your company. If you can build reseller-ready tools, your company's profit margins will improve, directly impacting its bottom line – and make you look good.
- *Set up a hotline* with the reseller's support management to ensure good communication with your reseller partner. Hold regular meetings to exchange best practices.

"Past Due" Customers

If you work with external customers, there is one other group you should pay attention to, because your Chief Financial Officer is. These are customers who aren't paying their bills on time[2]. Of particular interest to you are any non-paying customers who are also consuming your support resources.

Work out a system between your team and the collections department so that you always have up-to-date lists of customers or resellers (and their customers) that are delinquent. This will allow you to flag these customers and set up an appropriate response when they do contact you.

Example: Thanks to newfound cooperation between the collections and support departments, a Fortune 100 company discovered that one of their support team's most demanding customers had not paid a bill in months! The support team gently informed the person calling for technical support that they were unable to help them until their long-overdue bill was paid. The customer paid up in full, and their support contract was quickly reinstated. It turned out to have been a simple clerical error in the customer's billing department, not an intentional attempt to avoid paying. A win-win resolution for everyone.

By the way, if your mental image of the collections department is a big guy with large muscles, you definitely need to visit them! They are masters of negotiation, not intimidation. Threats are not part of their vocabulary, except as a last resort.

Former Customers

Some of your best sources of intelligence are customers who are no longer your customers. Typically, they are very honest about why they left, if only someone asks them!

Interview every customer who chooses not to do business with you and discover their reasons. Share those reasons with management and make sure that your company learns from each of them.

In some larger companies, a senior executive is tasked with "win backs," i.e., bringing lapsed customers back as paying customers.

Frankly, not all customers are worth keeping, as you'll discover in Chapter 4, titled *Common Customer Support Myths*. But knowing why someone is no longer a customer can help you hold on to customers you do want to keep, before they slip away.

Psychology and Customer Service

A number of studies in behavioral science and psychology can assist us in better understanding customers. These studies illustrate concepts which can help us deliver better service.

Humans Need to See Improvement

Richard B. Chase and Sriram Dasu[3] offer some very interesting perspectives on customer service.

They cite a famous 1993 experiment in which subjects had to choose between two unpleasant experiences. In the first, subjects put their hands in uncomfortably cool water (57° F) for 60 seconds. In the second experiment, the same subjects put their hands in 57° degree water for 60 seconds – followed by an additional 30 seconds in slightly warmer water (59° F).

Even though the second experiment lasted 50% longer, almost three-quarters (70%) of the subjects stated they would rather repeat the longer, 90 second experience rather than the first. Why? Because in the second experiment, the subjects could discern the improvement in comfort.

How does this relate to customer service? Remember that people have an innate urge to see improvement. When you are working through issues with customers, remember that they don't always expect things to be fixed immediately. They can tolerate some delays as long as they see that you are making progress. Demonstrate that you genuinely care about resolving the issue. Show your customers that things are improving.

Finish Strong

Another important principle to keep in mind as you design your service experiences is to finish strong. People tend to remember the end of an experience more than any other part. If you ever visit a Disney theme park, for example, you'll notice that "cast members" (their term for employees) spend a lot of time reminding you where you parked your car. ("Remember, you're parked in Section G for Goofy.") Why? They know that even if your kids have a great time with Mickey and friends, their screams of joy will be replaced by your screams of frustration if you cannot find your car in the hundreds of acres of parking lots.

Here's another example of the "Finish Strong" principle in action:

Thanksgiving holidays are the busiest travel time in the USA. During a recent Thanksgiving trip, I was concerned that a smaller airport that I don't normally use would run out of parking spaces. It had happened before, and I didn't want to repeat the experience. So I researched off-airport parking options. I found a company that not only guaranteed parking (without a reservation); they promised that a shuttle would come around every 5 minutes to take customers to the airport terminals.

Everything worked as promised. Even though chaos reigned in the airport, our off-airport parking experience was very pleasant. We had a wonderful holiday, but "where-the-heck-did-I-park" panic momentarily set in when we picked up our baggage and tried to remember what we had done with the car. What *was* the name of the off-airport parking company?

Then I remembered that the driver had given us a wallet-sized slip with the name and contact information of the parking service – along with the row number that our car was parked in! A happy ending! What could have been a great experience marred by a sloppy ending turned out to be a very pleasant one. And they now have a loyal customer.

Give Customers Choice, But Not Too Much

A fascinating article in the *International Journal of Personality and Social Psychology*[4] shed some interesting light on choice and stress.

This article showed that *moderate* levels of choice and information are optimal for coping with stress. For example, if a nurse lets a patient choose which arm to draw blood from, the patient is happier and far more satisfied than if they're not offered a choice.

In this example, giving the customer a choice makes no difference at all to the service provider. The blood quality is the same in either arm. But having a choice makes a big difference to the customer. It increases their satisfaction with the service provider. Having a choice gives customers some degree of control over the interaction, which invariably improves their satisfaction. Even when customers feel helpless, they still like to have some control over the outcome, even if that control is only symbolic.

But be careful not to give customers too many choices! You have probably experienced this personally when you were really hungry and trying to decide what to eat. If the menu has a seemingly endless set of options and variations, all deliciously described in mouth-watering detail, what happens? You take a long time to decide, flip-flopping between different options before settling in on your choice – often an old favorite. Too much choice paralyzes!

Lessons Learned from the Medical World

As you might imagine, there has been interesting research to find out why certain doctors have more malpractice suits[5] filed against them than others. The reasons are not only doctor negligence or error, but also the quality of the communication between the doctor and the patient.

Primary care physicians who had no previous malpractice claims against them were more likely to have significantly longer visits with patients, use humor and ask patients for their opinions. I suspect there are many lessons to be learned from this research in the support world, particularly as companies push hard to bring down their average call handle time, i.e., time they speak with a customer.

Speculation Becomes Fact

Speculating on a possible solution before knowing the actual cause of a problem is dangerous. It can damage a service encounter. You have probably seen this – most likely from someone who has good service instincts, but little training.

This scenario typically happens like this: A sympathetic support person is listening to a customer's tale of woe, and says, "I suspect it may be X, but we'll have to look at it more to be sure."

This offhand comment could be the kiss of death for this particular service encounter. No matter what turns out to be the actual cause, your customer will remember your speculations and fixate on them as the cause, particularly if you cannot find a solution quickly.

The lesson: While you are still investigating the root cause of an issue, it is far better not to speculate.

Keep in Touch with Your Customers

With the highly interrupt-driven nature of your job, who has time to reach out to customers on a proactive basis? Is reaching out to customers really worth it? Yes! It is much cheaper to keep or upgrade a current customer than it is to acquire a new one. Once you acquire a customer, support plays a vital role in keeping profitable customers for life.

If you rely solely on your website to keep customers up to date on new offerings, you are missing out on multiple opportunities to enhance your customer relationships. No matter how good your website is, few customers are likely to go out of their way looking for your new services or latest offerings. Think about your own life. You may really enjoy your car or your latest set of golf clubs. There is a good chance you researched these relatively high-ticket items online before you bought them. But since you made your purchase, how often have you been back to the manufacturer's site? Not very often, I suspect.

Another good reason to maintain contact with customers on an ongoing basis is personnel changes. Chances are, the people who originally saw a need and purchased your product or service have since either moved on to other jobs or even left the company. You need to cultivate a relationship with the people now occupying their chairs.

There are many ways to keep in touch with your customers. Some of the more popular methods are discussed below.

Customer Satisfaction Surveys

Customer surveys breed satisfaction. A 2002 *Harvard Business Review* article[6] by Paul Dholakia and Viki Morowitz showed that after one year, customers who were surveyed about service satisfaction were three times more likely to open a new account. They were also half as likely to defect and were more profitable than customers who had not been surveyed.

> *Note:* The only difference between the two groups was that one had been surveyed. Neither group received any direct marketing from the company during the year.

There are three types of customer satisfaction surveys:

1. A one time, *ad-hoc* survey to answer a particular question from, say, customer support or product development.

2. A *transactional* survey that is a brief survey after the conclusion of an event, e.g., a service call. It would be analogous to a quality control check in manufacturing. A transactional survey is typically supplemented by a periodic survey.

3. *A periodic* survey where the questions may focus on the overall relationship and things that occur less frequently, such as a contract renewal.

Response rates, experts say, depend on your relationship with the customer. While there is no such thing as a "good" response rate, the following rates are common:

- Postal mail-based survey: 10–20% response rate
- Telephone-based survey: 50% response rate
- Web-based survey: 25% response rate

One expert on surveys is Professor Fred Van Bennekom, author of *Customer Surveying: A Guidebook for Service Managers.*[7] Van Bennekom shared his best practices for surveys:

- A survey deserves the same focus and project management as a product launch. In the customer service environment, surveys are too often done without resources – a "spare time" type of project. That is a recipe for disaster. For a customer service organization that is "fire fighting" in nature, a survey will invariably be pushed to the back burner and not properly designed or resourced.
- Be sure to pilot the survey so that you can work out the bugs and understand what works within your environment and for your customer base.
- Don't rely too much on open-ended questions, because you may not be able to take action on the responses entered. Open-ended questions are questions that require more than a "yes" or "no" answer. Analyzing open-ended questions is difficult. They are time-consuming to tabulate and summarize.
- Minimize respondent burden. Make it easy and pleasant for them to participate in the survey.

Remember, a survey is supposed to find out how effective you are in the eyes of the customer. Focusing on purely internal measures only reveals half of the story. Many surveys only ask for information on things they can use to run their operations better. Don't forget to determine the *outcomes* – what the customer got out of the interaction.

Newsletters

One of the most effective and least expensive ways to reach out to your customers and reseller partners on a regular basis is via newsletters. Newsletters deliver a lot of value. They can be an effective means of keeping your customers, resellers and distributors informed about what is going on. They let you spread the word about new product and service offerings, and keep your company's name in the customer's awareness.

Planning and implementing a newsletter is far beyond the scope of this book, but here are a few suggestions. First, target a single audience and make sure it delivers information which that audience values. Don't try to be all things to all audiences. Decide on either a print or email format (or both). How often should your newsletter go out (weekly, monthly, quarterly)?

In larger companies, the marketing and/or corporate communications departments may own all outbound customer communications. Be sure to check with them first before attempting to launch a newsletter or any sort of outbound campaign. They are also the ones who will provide guidance and assistance with the "look and feel" of the newsletter – corporate logos, official fonts, company style guide, etc. Seek their input and assistance.

Putting together a newsletter requires hard work and commitment. It also demands fresh content for each issue. This can be made a little easier by creating various departments or columns that appear in each issue, then soliciting contributions for each from appropriate department heads or staff members. Here are a few possibilities:

- *Spotlight* a different group or department in each issue.
- *Executive's Corner* could feature company or industry leaders talking about issues that would interest a wide audience.

- *Top Support Tips* could include information and solutions for the latest issues facing customers.
- *Upcoming Events* could showcase new products and services, reminders of things to be done (e.g., passwords that need to be reset periodically, etc.)
- *Customer Focus* could showcase how one particular customer is using your product or service in an innovative way.

Tips:

- If you are sending an email newsletter, choose your email subject line and content carefully to avoid spam filters.
- Create a separate "From/Reply to" address, and then ask subscribers to add it to their address books.
- Take care to ensure that you meet, at a minimum, all appropriate privacy and anti-spam laws.
- Be sure to offer subscribers an easy way to unsubscribe in every issue.

Readers and others interested in the latest developments in customer service and support are invited to subscribe to my free global service delivery newsletter, The Verghis View, by visiting my website.[8]

RSS Feeds

An increasingly popular method for distributing information and alerting people about additions to a website is called Real Simple Syndication (RSS). This format allows subscribers to get summaries of regularly changing web content.

RSS feeds enable readers to receive news, blog headlines and more, far more quickly and easily than by visiting each website individually. The content doesn't arrive in the customer's email inbox, nor do readers visit a series of websites. Instead, RSS feeds are accessed using special newsreader software, which until fairly recently excluded many mainstream web users. But now many websites and portals, including *My Yahoo!,* can receive RSS feeds and display them in your web browser. Like newsletters, readers can subscribe or unsubscribe from an RSS feed at any time.

Customer support would be a wonderful place to implement an RSS feed. Like the rest of us, your customers are probably drowning in email. A customer support RSS feed could notify customers or resellers about changes in your website, system notifications, updates and new features, all without the customer having to visit your website.

User Conferences

If you have a product or service that your customers can modify and build on, you probably will benefit from a user conference.

User conferences are excellent forums for customers and company staff to mingle. Your team will learn more about how customers use your products or service, and you can inform them about your company's latest offerings and future plans. Conferences provide valuable "face time" between employees and customers, and among customers themselves. Conferences enable customers to develop a more personal, visceral connection with your company than online or telephone connections ever could. And that personal connection breeds customer loyalty.

Some executives get nervous about the idea of a user conference. They fear unhappy customers will attend and gang up on the company. Frankly, if this is your worry, then you may have something to worry about. Perhaps the quality of your product or service, not to mention your relationships with customers, should be examined realistically. And don't forget, an unhappy customer can be your best and most honest source of information, particularly if they don't have an axe to grind – and especially if they think you might improve the situation. Remember what we mentioned earlier about people needing to see improvement?

Think about it. Wouldn't you rather have potentially unpleasant conversations occur in a setting where you can do something about a problem – rather than let them happen without your knowledge?

Your user conference should include a full slate of customer presentations. Just remember, this is not a hard-sell opportunity. Present information of value and interest. Show respect for the attendee's time. Make sure there's a heavy turnout of your top management team at the conference. Make them visible and available.

Sales-Support Marketing Tours

A combined sales and support marketing tour is essentially a mini-version of a user conference, but can be arranged with much less effort. Partner with your sales team to develop a city/regional "tour." Have your regional sales team invite existing customers and prospects for a day of meetings.

During the tour, feed them well. Introduce topics of interest to them. Be sure to give customers a chance to speak. The basic tenets are the same as at user conferences. Reach out to customers and prospects and build relationships, while receiving valuable feedback at the same time.

Customer Advisory Boards

Companies have boards of directors, universities have boards of trustees. Why shouldn't customer support have a high-level advisory board guiding them?

A Customer Advisory Board (CAB) comprises senior level executives from your customer base (or, if you provide only internal support, senior managers from the departments you support). Ask them for honest feedback on your services. Their input will help you validate your service vision and roadmap in a meaningful way.

Unfortunately, it's difficult to coax senior executives to join your board. Ask anyone who is trying to fill board vacancies.

And once you get the group started, you will have to work hard to keep other groups from taking over ownership of managing the board because of the value they provide to your company.

Who Should Be on the CAB?

External customer advisory boards should include a representative sample of your customer base. If your company targets vertical market segments, recruit representatives from those verticals, e.g., financial, technology, web-centric, government, educational, international, etc.

If you are not familiar with the profiles of your current customers (or target customers), contact your product management or sales team. Since they know the product pipeline as well as the revenue mix from existing products, either one can help you determine who should be on the board.

Remember, you want to invite support executives and CIOs to be on the board. They have the right perspective on support, i.e., not right on the front lines, but close enough to understand what is going on.

It's natural to want to recruit people that really like you or your company. This is not a bad thing, but don't go overboard. Invite at least a few people or companies who dislike your company, or who have been disappointed from a service perspective. These are the ones who can teach you the most. In addition, get people who challenge you and your teams to do better. The only type of person you *don't* want on your CAB is someone who is just taking up space, and not participating fully in the board's activities.

> *Tip:* Be sure to seek out influential people, individuals that others listen to. In his book *Tipping Point: How Little Things Can Make a Big Difference,* author Malcolm Gladwell calls these people "connectors." These people can do an extraordinary job pulling people together – exactly what you want on your CAB.

If you're forming an internal group, the concept is similar. Get a representative sampling of departments you provide service to, and invite their senior people to be on the board. Since they're within your own company, you should know the players, and be able to request the specific people you want on the CAB.

How to Get the Most Value from a CAB

Make sure that being asked to join your CAB is seen as a prestigious appointment, one that is earned by the quality of the input they provide.

To keep the board fresh and new ideas flowing, make sure there's enough turnover. Allow two years for the first CAB board, then rotate one-third of the members off the board each year.

Board members should understand that they are expected to participate, in order to remain on the board. Just showing up is not enough. Board members should get homework (not too much, but enough for their plane flight) and be required to arrive prepared for meetings.

At the same time, be sure to give them enough time to socialize with each other and senior executives from your company. This is where a lot of good ideas – and future revenue – will come from.

Finally, remind CAB members that they are there to give *input*, not to vote on final direction. At each meeting, encourage a member of your CAB to talk about their strategic initiatives. This will be educational for the rest of the CAB as well as valuable input for you.

What Do They Get Out of It?

The biggest perk of being a CAB member should be the opportunity to network with other senior support executives. Serving on a CAB should be perceived as a prestigious appointment. Ask your marketing people to prepare and distribute a press release profiling each company representative who becomes a CAB member.

For members representing an external company, being on your CAB allows them to give input on the future service direction of your company. They also get access to your company's top executives, and knowledge of future development and support plans.

How Often Should CABs Meet?

Meetings should be held at least once a year, with quarterly meetings by conference call. Do not have the once-a-year-in-person meeting during your annual sales conference or during any other event where internal staff are distracted. Give CAB members your total attention.

4 Common Customer Support Myths

The great enemy of the truth is very often not the lie – deliberate, contrived and dishonest – but the myth – persistent, persuasive and unrealistic.

– John F. Kennedy, former US President

There are many persistent myths about customer service, and over the years I've been dismayed to hear them repeated by otherwise intelligent service professionals.

Myth: The Customer is Always Right

This statement has been repeated so often, it is assumed to be the truth. Unfortunately, it is not. Customers are human and full of the same frailties that afflict all humans. Some of them lie, some cheat, some take out completely unrelated frustrations on you. If you are nodding your head in agreement, you know exactly what I am talking about. I'd modify that statement slightly to say, "The customer is *almost* always right."

Early in my career, I worked at the University of New Hampshire, which was partially funded by the state government. As a member of second-level support, I had a call escalated to me one day from one of the front line help desk staff.

On the phone was a lawyer from one of the larger cities in New Hampshire. This gentleman was upset because the partially *state-funded* university would not send someone to his office to remove a virus from his computer. He was not a member of the university community, and admitted that the virus did not come from anyone in the university community. He would not listen to the help desk staff member who had explained we were only able to assist university faculty, staff and students.

Our philosophy at UNH was that everyone was a customer, at least for the first few minutes. If it became clear that they weren't part of the university community, we would refer them to an appropriate commercial company.

When I got on the phone, I offered him a number of possible alternatives. I even offered to set up an appointment with a computer services company that was right down the street from his office. He did not like any of the alternatives, and started getting angrier and more verbally abusive as the call progressed.

I tried reasoning with him. I pointed out that if we helped everyone in the state just because we were partially taxpayer-funded, it would be unfair competition to commercial computer service operations. They couldn't compete with our "state subsidy." How would you feel, I asked, if the university started offering free legal services in your firm's specialty – in direct competition with you?

Realizing the call was going nowhere, I decided to end it this way. "There is an air force base near you, isn't that right, sir?"

"Yes, but what the *@%# does that have to do with this conversation?" he snapped.

"Well, the Air Force is 100% taxpayer-funded," I replied. "If you can convince them to fly you and your computer down to our campus, I will personally remove any and all viruses from your computer. If not, here is the name and number of a computer service provider on your street."

Click.

I'm sure the man must have had other issues going on to cause such a momentary lapse of reason and manners. But there was no reason for the staff or me to take that abuse. We had other legitimate customers that were waiting to be helped.

In a non-profit situation like that one, it is even more important to clearly understand your customer base, and marshal your scarce resources towards them and them alone. Not everyone who asks you for help, after all, is a customer.

Myth: They Pay Us a Lot; They Must Be Good Customers

As companies mature and their service goes from good to great, they often end up providing great service – but to the wrong customer.

Sometimes your "best" customers aren't who you think they are. A common myth is believing that your best customers are the ones who bring in the most revenue. That seems obvious. Unfortunately, it's often not true – and can lead to throwing away good money. Here's why.

Often the clients that pay the most have also negotiated the biggest discounts. So they may not generate as much profit as you think. In addition, these customers often consume a disproportionate amount of your company's resources. Naturally, everyone wants to keep these "important" customers happy.

Step back. Sit down with your financial team and review the numbers. You may be surprised to discover the correlation between revenue and profit. Often your biggest revenue sources are *not* your most profitable customers. Uncover the facts, and then adjust your service accordingly. After all, you do want your company to stay in business, right?

Myth: All Customers Expect Great Service

As customer support professionals, we assume that all customers expect great service. This is simply not true. If you think it is, you may be squandering scarce resources on people who do not value great service.

Examine your customer base. Understand exactly why each customer buys your products or services, and why they choose to stay with your company. Then you can adjust service levels to match their preferences.

Let's look at three common categories of customer service types.

Many of your top customers probably expect extensive hand-holding in return for all the money they pay you. If that's the case, be sure to pamper them, and make extra efforts to build an in-person relationship with them. They're paying a bundle for the best service you can provide.

But there's another category of customer, the "Don't call me, I'll call you" type. This customer also expects high standards of service – she just doesn't want to pay a lot for it. This customer is likely to be highly skilled in what they do, know exactly what they want, and will hold your team to the same high standards they hold themselves to. For this type of customer, you'd be wise to provide easy-to-use, do-it-yourself tools, combined with the option to call in and have a customer service rep walk them through the process whenever they deem it necessary.

Then there's the third type of customer, the "no frills" type. These customers are probably too small to get great service from anyone, so even a little effort on your part will go a long way toward building loyalty and satisfaction. They're probably comfortable with the "Pay as you go" support model.

My point is this: If you expend your limited resources trying to provide outstanding service to *all* your customers – even those who don't value it – you will most likely be forced to give less than great service to everyone.

Myth: Your Customer and Your Contact Have the Same Priorities

When interacting with customers, it's natural to spend time cultivating contacts at that company. You're looking for insight into their priorities and opinions. You need information and guidance about what is going on, so you can better serve them. A good contact can supply that information.

But it's a mistake to assume that what your contact wants from customer support is what the company itself wants. In rare instances – for employees who actually put the company's interests ahead of their own – that may be true. But in many cases, it's not.

Again, it's important to step back. Remember, particularly in larger institutions, that you're dealing with an individual, not an entire company. Understand the motivations of that individual, and realize that what they say may not be in complete alignment with their company's true needs and goals. Be prepared to seek out different viewpoints. Gently challenge your contact if you suspect that what they say doesn't represent their company's real interests. If you don't, you may end up implementing strategies that don't yield the results you expect. After all, they're aimed at satisfying the individual, not the company he represents.

5 People

People often say that motivation doesn't last. Well, neither does bathing - that's why we recommend it daily.

– Zig Ziglar, author, motivational speaker

The quality of your staff is the single biggest predictor of your team's success. Payroll is also typically the single biggest line item in your budget. Spend as much time as necessary and as much money as you can afford on the people part of your business. It will pay off in a big way *en route* to you becoming an Ultimate Customer Support Executive.

Staffing

You have undoubtedly heard that the three foundations of successful support are *people, process* and *technology* in that order. That's what the experts say, and they're right. Specifically:

- *Hire the right people*, always trading up as you need to replace.
- *Tap into the knowledge* of the bright people you hire. Let them build the right customer-centric processes (which includes discarding bad processes), then
- *Implement the right set of technologies* that enable you to make your customer support strategy a reality.

How Many People Do You Really Need?

You have a problem. Your team is overworked. Customers frequently complain that they can't get through to support. You know you need more staff, and perhaps more phone lines. But how many? How do you calculate how many people and phone lines you really need?

One solution is obvious and simple – and wrong. Let's say that on average, you get 100 incoming phone calls[1] every hour. Each call takes an average of 3 minutes to resolve. At that rate, one person should be able to handle 20 calls an hour. So you need 5 people and 5 phone lines to handle all 100 calls, right?

Wrong.

The problem is, customers do not call at precise intervals and speak for exactly the same length of time in every call. Virtually all support centers have two distinct daily peaks of incoming queries: a morning rush, followed by a smaller mid-afternoon peak. Staff can't be on the phone all day, or they are likely to burn out. They have to take periodic breaks.

When determining how many phone lines you actually need, don't forget to include your team's *outgoing* calls to other groups to resolve issues. At universities, this number could be as high as 30% of the incoming calls.

In a world where incoming queries don't arrive in a nice predictable sequence, how do you calculate the number of people and phone lines you really need? The ideal solution will maximize the number of customer support people on the phone helping customers, while minimizing the length of time a caller must wait to talk to a customer support person.

Calculating the correct answer doesn't take IBM's *Big Blue* supercomputer. In fact, a Danish scientist named Agner Erlang figured out the answer almost a century ago, and is the basis for almost all workforce scheduling programs, described in more detail in Chapter 6, titled *Technology*.

Hiring

What kind of person should you hire? The answer is very simple. Hire the very best person you can afford, even for the lower-paid, front lines positions.

Why? Every support person is the face of your organization to the customer. Each is expected to have in-depth knowledge about your organization and its services, and to resolve most issues during the first contact (if it is not already taken care of before the customer even realizes something is wrong).

Customers are already frustrated when they call, and their unhappiness increases whenever an issue must be escalated from the front lines to another team for resolution. It is also potentially more expensive for your company. In most companies, the lower paid generalists are considered "Tier 1" or "front-line" support. The group they escalate problems to is called "Tier 2." This group is typically shielded from direct contact with customers, and deals instead with escalations and special projects. Beyond that is often a "Tier 3" support, which typically includes the developer level team, either inside the company or outside.

Each level of support is paid considerably more than the tier below it. As problems escalate up the ladder of support, consider the hourly wage differential, not to mention the opportunity cost of your higher-level resources. It's always less expensive to have problems resolved by a front-line person. So hire the very best you can afford.

Another age-old question is: which kind of person should you hire for your customer support team? Do you look for people with the technical skills, and then teach them how to interact well with customers? Or do you recruit those with good "people skills" and help them master the necessary technical skills?

The consensus is the latter. Experience has shown that that it's easier to hire a person with good people skills and train them technical skills, than to teach a technical person people skills. This is true even in very complex technical support environments. At Akamai, for example, we had people with MS degrees and even PhDs on the front lines[2] of technical support. Customer support recruited from the same pool as Engineering and R&D. If they loved working with customers, they were hired into customer support. If they loved working with customers, but from a distance, they were sent to Engineering.

What qualities should you look for in customer service staffers?

You want to hire the kind of person who enjoys working with people, has outstanding communication skills, can handle constant interruptions and multi-tasks exceptionally well. They should also handle stress well and be very detail-oriented. The best customer service performers can think on their feet, and often enjoy doing puzzles. On top of all that, they need an aptitude for technology, at least if they're providing technical support.

Who Does the Interviews?

In a customer support environment, your staff members depend on each other a great deal. As manager, you'll probably interact with your team much less frequently than they'll interact with each other.

So why is it that in almost all cases, managers are the only ones who do the interviewing? Why do managers alone make the "hire/no hire" decision? Why not have your team make the decision, with your input being one of the factors they consider?

Naturally, you must guide the team to ensure they interview and evaluate candidates properly. Confer with your Human Resources department to make sure that your team stays within legal constraints. For example, in the US you cannot ask questions about an applicant's age, marital status or ethnic heritage.

> *Personal example:* At Akamai, we asked team members to keep two criteria in mind as they interviewed candidates. One was the "cubicle test" which asked, if you had to share a cubicle with this person for 3 months, would you like it? Or would he or she drive you crazy?
>
> The second criterion was to hire people you liked, but who were not like you. This prevented us from

overlooking people who were very good, but perhaps had unorthodox backgrounds or styles. This also reduced the chance for "groupthink" down the road.

Hmmm, I Should Know That

One of the paradoxes in life is that the better you know something, the harder it is to explain it to someone else.

At Akamai, one of the questions we asked candidates for our external technical support team was how to tie shoelaces. The catch? The person making the request was visually impaired and making the request via the phone.

Most candidates got completely flummoxed trying to answer this question.

What we wanted to see was how a person reacted to an unusual request, particularly about something the candidate could literally do with their eyes closed. We were interested in seeing how they reached a possible solution, and how comfortable they were asking follow-up questions and contextual questions of the person making the unusual request.

Wouldn't You Like To Hire This Person?

I've heard several variations of the following story, which is also recounted in Peter Greenberg's *Travel Detective*.[3] The story unfolds in an airport, where there are long lines to talk to the gate agent.

A rather aggressive gentleman pushes his way to the front of a long queue. He tells the ticket agent, "I would like you to help me now." The agent answers very politely, "Sir, I'm afraid you are going to have to wait in line."

The man gets belligerent, and continues to demand attention. He yells, "Do you know who I am?"

The agent calmly picks up the microphone and addresses the crowd. "Ladies and gentleman, there is a well dressed gentleman at Gate Two who doesn't know who he is. Can anyone help him out, please?"

The man grows even angrier and tells the female gate agent to do an anatomically impossible task. The agent calmly replies, "I'm sorry, sir. You're going to have to wait in line for that, too!"

This story has brought chuckles to just about every customer support person I know because they wish they could think on their feet like this. I'm sure many would like to put some of their particularly troublesome customers in their place like this woman did.

Understanding and Motivating Your Team

With all the lip service given to putting customers first, and the importance of customer loyalty, you'd think that customer support would be a wonderful place to work. Unfortunately, this is not the case today. In fact, in most companies this is so far from the truth, it is worth examining why.

First, support as a profession is one of the few areas where people call only with a problem or complaint. No one ever calls to say, "I love you guys. You're doing a great job. Everything's working just fine, and I just wanted thank you."[4] When you work in customer support, you expect to deal with a constant barrage of unhappy people. Still, it is hard to cope with, day in and day out.

Second, there's a huge disconnect between what corporate executives *say* and what they *do*. Some executives look at support as merely a cost center, an expensive necessity. They don't see it offering much added value. Some executives even see support professionals as merely protecting the company from unhappy customers. These executives fail to see the support function as a profession, nor do they consider the people who fulfill that function as important contributors.

These mistaken attitudes are likely to drive down customer satisfaction and cost the company dearly in terms of customer loyalty and retention. After all, if the people helping customers are not happy themselves, it's hard to imagine them making the customers happy.

Personality Inventory Indicators

Once you have hired your support team, a personality inventory test can help you see how different people absorb and process information. There are a number of well-known personality inventory programs. The most popular is the Myers-Briggs Type Indicators (MBTI), which is administered to some 2.5 million people each year.[5]

Its goal is to help people work more successfully in teams. General Electric's famous leadership school in Groton, Connecticut, USA has used it for years.

The basic premise behind MBTI is that people receive, process, and act upon information in different ways. Psychologist Carl Jung, whose work was the foundation Myers-Briggs built on, postulated that behavior can be explained by differences in how people:

- Focus their attention – extraverted (E) or introverted (I)
- Take in information – by sensing (S) or intuiting (N)
- Make decisions – by thinking (T) or feeling (F)

Isabel Briggs-Myers added a fourth criterion.

- How people relate to the outside world – by judging (J) or perceiving (P)

Combining these four attributes yields 16 different personality types. Administering this test to your staff may help you understand how each one processes information, and help you communicate in a way that they best understand.

Most IT professionals, according to *CIO Magazine* columnist Susan Cramm,[6] are INTJs (Introverted, Intuitive, Thinking, Judging). INTJs typically are imaginative and determined innovators, stimulated by difficulties and attracted to bigger and bigger challenges.

Career Anchors

Since many front-line customer support staff are relatively young and inexperienced, how do you help them make career choices? One influential concept is that of "career anchors," developed by Edgar Schein[7] from MIT's Sloan School of Business.

Schein believes that career anchors shape what we do and the choices we make. People have a particular preference for one over the others. For example, a person whose primary theme is Security/Stability will seek secure and stable employment over, say, employment that is challenging and riskier. People tend to stay anchored in one area, he says, and their career will echo this in many ways.

Discovering what motivates and stimulates people, their so-called career anchors, can help you understand how people perceive risk/reward in their careers. Schein defines eight career anchors:

- Technical/functional competence
- General managerial competence
- Autonomy/independence
- Security/stability
- Entrepreneurial creativity
- Sense of service
- Pure challenge
- Lifestyle

In my experience, the key motivations for many people in the customer support fields are technical/ functional competence and a sense of service. Technical/functional people like being good at something and will work to become a guru or expert. They like challenges and using their skill to meet the challenge. They enjoy doing a job properly and performing better than almost anyone else.

Succession Planning

Now that you have hired a great team and used a variety of tools to help you understand how they prefer to work, the next step is to get started deciding who will take your place.

Succession planning is one of the most overlooked and underrated parts of any position, particularly in customer support. Most of us are too busy doing our jobs and managing our careers to think seriously about succession planning. Big mistake!

If you do a good job as a customer support executive, you will touch just about every department in your company. When you get a promotion and your team begins to fall apart after you leave, you have failed as a leader! At the very least, your team should work just as well after your time leading them has ended. Ideally, they'll be even better. In a team environment, no individual can be greater than the team.

Succession planning has many advantages. From the organization's perspective, it gives them a deep pool of potential managerial talent. From the employee's perspective, it provides a career path.

Think about it another way. How else are you going to get promoted? After all, if no one is qualified to take your job, you are not likely to be asked to take on any additional responsibilities.

Develop a clear succession plan for each of your managers, and build in training that will allow them succeed in their new roles.

Ranking Employees

One of the more difficult things to do, particularly when you have a good team, is to rank your employees. I can hear you protest now. "I can't do that. They are all important in different ways." You are absolutely right!

But what if you had the chance to reward an employee – or were forced to make painful choices and eliminate someone? Don't you owe it to each member of your team to ensure that their entire contribution is taken into account, not just what is top of your mind at the time the decision has to be made?

At least once a quarter, I'd recommend you spend some time ranking each of your employees, from best to worst. It is much easier to review their contributions (and failures) once a quarter, than to do it once a year.

It can be especially tricky ranking employees across different functions. How do you determine if Jane in Technical Support is more valuable to the organization than Joe in Training?

> *Tip:* Rank employees within their functional area on the following criteria: indispensability to organization, difficulty of replacing individual, attitude, teamwork and potential. Of course, your criteria may vary. The important thing is to ensure that your approach is consistent and makes sense in terms of what you are trying to achieve.

Firing

One of the toughest things for any manager to do is to let someone go. It is particularly hard for support managers, since most of us are attracted to this profession because we care about people and enjoy helping them.

Everyone deserves a second chance, of course. You owe it to the people who are not performing to advise them when they are not measuring up, and to give them every opportunity to improve. At the same time you must hold them accountable for their performance. If they clearly understand what is expected of them and still cannot reach the standards you have set, you must let them go.[8]

Don't succumb to the temptation to find them another role and transfer them to another department. It is completely unacceptable to shift the problem around. If they do not meet the requirements of the job they have been hired to do, you have no business foisting them off on some other part of the company. You must deal with the situation and let the employee go.

On the other hand, if the person has met all the requirements for the job for which they are hired, and they want to move to another department, then by all means actively find a more suitable job for them in the company.

You owe it to the customer and the company to get the right people "on the bus" – by hiring them – and get the wrong people "off the bus" – by firing them. Most support executives spend too much time cleaning up messes created by people who are no longer the right fit for the customer support team. They should be spending their time cultivating the good people or making the OK ones better.

I strongly recommend doing all firings in person, particularly if the people were managed remotely. Termination is a difficult task. You should look people in the eye and let them know exactly what is happening and why, as well as the next steps. They may not like the message. But if you have done your job correctly, they would have had multiple opportunities to correct their shortcomings, it should not come as a surprise to them.

Tip: If you find that you frequently have to fire relatively new hires, you should inspect the situation carefully. Among other possibilities, something may be wrong with your interviewing process, your training may be inadequate or the environment is not friendly to new employees.

Layoffs

If anything is more difficult than firing someone whose work has been unsatisfactory, it is letting people go when their performance has been exemplary. Layoffs commonly occur after mergers or consolidations. An office shuts down, or the business is not doing as well as expected and needs to reduce headcount. While layoffs haven't been as common outside the US, this is changing with rapid globalization.

A layoff is another one of those instances when you have to think about the company first, then your team second. What makes it particularly difficult for those of us in support is that we tend to be a close-knit community. We usually know each other well and are friends.

If you do have to lay off people, they are probably going to be shocked. During the termination meeting, spend the necessary time to let them know the reasons for the layoff, and offer all the support you can. If you are allowed to,[9] offer to be a reference for them.

As you tell the affected people the bad news, start notifying those who will be staying that they are safe. Explain why layoffs were necessary and the rationale for their staying. Let them know when all affected employees have been informed and the layoff has ended.

Coordinate with Human Resources to ensure that everyone is consistent in their answers, and knows what to do or say when questions or uncomfortable situations come up.

Since support groups interact with customers, it is quite possible that outsiders will call to ask what is going on. Be sure that a single consistent message, approved by the company or marketing department, has been created and is delivered to any outsiders who ask about the layoffs. Assure customers that plans are in place to ensure that there is no disruption in support.

What Happens When *You* Get Fired or Laid Off?

As you rise through the ranks, you will realize an awful truth. The longevity of your career in a company is less about what you have done in the past than what you can do for them in the future. In other words, your career is like the price of a stock. It is based on future expectations, not how well you did last quarter or last year.

You may have done a phenomenal job in the past, but frankly, that is not relevant to your future with the organization. It is quite possible that you and the company have moved in different directions.

Don't get upset if this happens to you. Exit with class and grace. Don't burn any bridges. Don't say or do anything you might regret down the line.

People Tips

Given how much importance we place on the people side of the equation, there are a number of things that may seem counterintuitive unless you have had a chance to think it through.

Hero Complex

Congratulations. You have a "star" support person on your team. You know the one I'm talking about: the hero. The person everyone in your team goes to for help. Customers actively seek her out. She can always be counted on to go out of her way to help. She is the one who gets a disproportionate amount of kudos and thank you notes.

You might wish your entire department was filled with people just like her, right? Be careful of what you wish for! In many ways, she could be a problem for you without your knowing it.

For example, if she is the only one fulfilling requests that are outside the scope of your team, then of course customers will start asking for her by name. No one else will do what she does! You may soon find that she is too busy to document the special things she does, or share the special knowledge she's acquired.

This is a great employee who is going bad – and it's probably happened with your unwitting encouragement! When an outstanding member of a team receives praise and rewards, others notice. If you consistently reward an individual over the team, people will begin hoarding what they know and not sharing it with others.

Encourage your heroes to share their knowledge and bring everyone up to the same high level of service. If one member is doing things that are always above and beyond, discover why. Have your procedures and policies become stale and musty? Do they need to be updated, made more customer friendly? Or is it that she just cannot say "no?"

The goal is to make *everyone* on your team heroes, not just one or two people.

If There's Time to Complain, There's Time to Fix It

Because support is so central to a company, your front-line staff probably already knows where customer-impacting issues (and quite possibly their solutions) lie. If they feel that they are not being listened to, your team will get frustrated.

One powerful way to remove this frustration is to empower them to smash any issues that stand in the way of an outstanding customer experience. As customer support representatives, they will be able to see many of the poor processes that typically put in place for the convenience of internal departments, not for the convenience of the customer. To do this, you will have to clearly inform the rest of the company that this is the charter for your team. You might need to get "buy in" from an executive sponsor, if you feel you do not have the clout to make this happen by yourself (yet).

Your support team often has to work with other departments. One of the best ways to help them really understand how another group works (and vice versa) is to have them become a liaison with the other department. This means being part of the other department's meetings and sharing information on what can be done to improve the customer's experience.

Before unleashing your staff as a liaison to other departments, prepare them. Give them group-specific tips to help them better understand how to work with the other team. Set clear success criteria. Treat this as a project, i.e., with a start and end date, and milestones along the way.

Remember that sending someone off to be a liaison with another group means time away from your team, and away from directly interfacing with your customers.

When I worked at Duke University's Office of Information Technology, we developed an innovative way to cope with our annual autumn dilemma – thousands of students all wanting to connect to the campus network as soon as they arrived. One year we launched a project called SWAT – Students with Access to Technology. To assist our regular support staff, SWAT recruited a group of technically trained students to help other students with particular computer problems during the peak back-to-school rush.

It was such a rousing success that the following year, we put two students – who had participated in SWAT the previous year and had the most suggestions – in charge of the program.

What a difference! The students were able to give us insights and feedback that the staff would not have gotten normally. We also received an approval rating greater than 90%.

> *Hint:* Be careful what you ask college students in open-ended surveys. One of my all-time favorite responses was, "Service was awesome! I'd like (name deleted) to be the father of my children."

The year after the students took a key leadership role in running SWAT, the program won *Network World's* User Excellence Award of the Year[10] – the first University ever to achieve that honor.

Get Comfortable with Being Uncomfortable

If you are truly focused on the customer, you must be proactive. Set aside time to shake things up and see if you're still as customer-centric as you think you are. Both you and your team better start getting comfortable with being uncomfortable.

It's easy to slip into an attitude of "If it ain't broke, don't fix it." But be careful. These days, even if it ain't broke, someone else will kick it up a notch – and steal your customers with better service.

Even when things seem to be going well – perhaps *particularly* when things seem to be going well – that's the time to look at ways to make every customer-facing process a little bit better. After all, when things aren't going as well, you will be too busy reacting to issues to have the time to improve customer-facing processes.

Change is inevitable, but few people enjoy it. But being prepared for it, even initiating it, is a lot less stressful than having change imposed on you from the outside.

Managing Younger Employees

During the course of my engagements with clients of The Verghis Group, several veteran managers have confessed to me that they have a hard time motivating younger employees – those under age 30 or so. Typical comments include:

- "They get bored easily."
- "They have a short attention span."
- "They spend a lot of time chatting online."

Several of the techniques discussed earlier, including career anchors and personality type indicators like MBTI, can be helpful when managing younger staff. These tools can help you discover what motivates young people, and how they process information. Both are useful in managing a team.

Let's also understand what motivates and drives some younger employees. Many, especially those living in affluent countries, have never known a world without the Internet. Real time communication with people around the world via email, Instant Messaging (IM) and SMS- (Short Message Service) enabled phones is second nature to many younger employees. They eagerly embrace new gadgets, technologies and avenues of communications.

Many of them can handle copious amounts of data, juggle multiple tasks at once, and need challenges to keep from getting bored.

These younger employees can be a great resource. They can help you assess and try out some of the newer technologies like blogs and RSS (Real Simple Syndication), described in Chapter 7, titled *Technology*.

But because they have grown up being bombarded with media advertisements, they're often suspicious of attempts to manipulate how they think. They may be cynical about your company's perspectives and policies. Include them in discussions about the team, and make them part of the solution. That will go a long way in alleviating their fears of manipulation.

When managing young people, there are particular lessons you can learn from the video game industry. For example, manufacturers know that a game must be intuitive enough to let a player get started without having to read the instructions.[11]

But once they're hooked on the game, the reverse is true. The game must get progressively more challenging to keep them interested. It must strike the right balance between being too difficult and too boring ("grinding").

So what can we learn from this? Younger employees are likely to be good at problem solving. After all, this is the essence of almost all video games. Give them challenging projects and get them engaged. Just make sure that you get them started on the right foot.

Factoid: In Japan, there's an expression for mobile-text message addicts who are exceptionally adept at using their thumbs for entering messages on their keypads – *OYA YUBI SEDAI* ("The Thumb Generation"). Rumor has it that they use their thumbs so well they sometimes use them to point at things – and even to ring doorbells.

Professional Certification

Most of the people currently managing support organizations were promoted through the ranks and have never managed before.

I'd recommend all support managers get certified in one of the staff certification programs mentioned below, particularly if you haven't managed a support center at a manager or director level before.

Staff Certification

Until relatively recently, there weren't any certifications for customer support staff. To fill the void, three organizations now offer certifications for front line staff, managers and directors. In alphabetical order they are:

- HDI – Formerly known as the Help Desk Institute[12]
- SSPA – Service and Support Professionals Association[13]
- STI Knowledge[14]

In addition, you can get Ultimate Customer Support Executive training based on this book, directly from The Verghis Group.[15]

Each program has different strengths and weaknesses. I'd recommend researching each one and deciding why you should get certified in one program versus the other.

Organizational Certification

In addition to your own individual certification, consider getting your organization's customer support certified.

Four certification programs for organizations are available, each with its pros and cons. COPC, for example, is mainly for high volume contact centers (specifically call centers, e-commerce and transaction processing operations).

- COPC[16]
- HDI[17]

- Service Strategies[18]
- STI Knowledge[19]

6 Process

There is surely nothing quite so useless as doing with great efficiency what should not be done at all.

– Peter F. Drucker, management guru

A process is a sequence of steps that result in a particular outcome. Consistent, replicable processes are the cornerstone of business efficiency, quality and consistency. If you cannot document your repeatable business processes, then in essence you don't have any. Instead, what you consider processes are mere suggestions, *ad hoc* procedures that quite possibly change from person to person, depending on who's implementing them.

In 2002, the IT research and advisory firm Gartner Group estimated that 80% of downtime for mission critical systems was due to human error, poor testing, bad changes and weak problem detection. In other words, poor processes.

Poor processes not only lead to low quality, they devour profits. Esteemed quality guru Joseph M. Juran estimated the cost of poor quality at 20-40% of a company's sales. For service industries, poor quality costs an estimated 20-30% of sales.

Most of us in the support world would agree that people and technology are important issues. Process is where many of us stumble. Companies that struggle with processes either become slavish devotees of process – to the detriment of common sense – or their processes are so poorly documented, they are an accident waiting to happen.

Unwritten processes are the worst. Like letters scrawled in sand, they change arbitrarily. Yet somehow they become codified into unwritten rules that cannot easily be examined, improved or optimized.

Processes must be documented!

A well documented set of processes helps you identify and resolve problems in your operation. Periodic review of these processes prevents them from becoming inflexible and archaic.

Here's another important thing to remember about processes: their higher purpose is always to help your business serve the customer. They are not merely for the convenience of your support organization. How many times have you heard someone from an organization say, "Sorry, that's not how we do things around here. That's not part of our procedure."

Processes used by internal and external customer support teams vary quite widely. Internal customer support teams are more likely to follow standard processes and frameworks than teams serving external customers. If you are already familiar with the processes listed below, feel free to skim over them. This is merely a high level overview. If you haven't seen them before, read them and see what makes sense to refer more to. In many cases be aware that others in your organization may already be familiar with the processes and frameworks described. There's no need to reinvent the wheel!

Before we get into different processes and frameworks, here are a few simple techniques that I have found that have helped me over the years. If you are overwhelmed with a problem, and don't know where to start, these are a good set of techniques.

Flowchart the processes – first from an internal point of view and then from a customer's point of view. Flowcharts make it much easier to visualize what is going on. Look carefully to see what steps can be eliminated. Which steps are only for the convenience of the organization, not the customer? Remove them!

If you have too many things to do and not enough time or resources to tackle them all, use pareto charts to see what the biggest issue is, or what has the most negative customer impact. A pareto chart helps you visually see what issues are being raised with the most frequency. In particular, the pareto chart helps you answer the following questions: *What are the biggest issues facing our team? Which 20% of issues are causing 80% of the problems? Where should we focus our efforts to achieve the greatest improvements?* Once you have the answers, start on those issues that give you the most return for your efforts *and* consider those efforts that will be most valued by your customers.

Another simple but often overlooked technique is to reach out to other groups that have similar issues and see if you can pool resources or share techniques to solve similar issues. For example, let's assume you are part of the central IT group at a university, and are in the process of a major overhaul to the online student registration process. Rather than attempt to train potentially thousands or even tens of thousands of students or wait for them to contact you in the inevitable rush right before they need to register, see who else you can enlist to help you. Groups that come to mind include the "ResNet" team that provides computer support to your students in their residence halls, the Resident Assistants that live in student housing and are there to guide students with their transition to university life, Student Government and the campus newspaper. All of these groups probably have good connections with students. Allowing them to help you can reduce the immense crush you have at the start of each school semester.

Overview of Best Practices, Frameworks and Standards

Let's start off with my definition of "best practices," "frameworks," "methodologies" and "standards." Then we'll look at some examples.

Best practice	The processes, practices, or systems widely recognized as improving an organization's performance and efficiency in specific areas.[1]
Standard	A process that has been ratified by a standards-defining body.
Framework	Guidance that is not prescriptive in nature. The framework tells you *who, what, where* and *when* to do something, but not *how* to do it.
Methodology	A certain approach or method of doing something. Not necessarily the best or only way. Often used by consultants promoting their particular solution to a company's woes.

In this chapter I will review some popular best practices, standards, frameworks and methodologies as they relate to customer service, particularly IT support. Then I will present one possible way they can be tied together to help your support department, even if it's not IT support, reach the next level of effectiveness.

Framework: Information Technology Infrastructure Library (ITIL)

In the last few years, ITIL[2] has become popular in the United States, quite a while after it swept across Europe.

ITIL documents best practices in the field of IT Service Management – that is, how to manage your tech support department as a business. Its approach is non-prescriptive, providing only advice and guidance on the key process and people issues involved in delivering IT services. ITIL was developed by the United Kingdom's Office of Government

Commerce[3] in conjunction with various practitioner and consulting organizations. In 2005, the OGC withdrew funding from ITIL, and the non-profit IT Service Management Forum[4] is now providing financing.

Following ITIL's guidance helps define the objectives, activities, inputs, and outputs of an IT support organization's processes. ITIL does not provide specific, detailed descriptions about how each process should be implemented. These will be different in each organization. Instead, ITIL recommends what an organization should do, but not how to do it.

In the early 1990s, ITIL published the first in what has become a series of eight books. The two most popular ones for IT Support professionals are *Service Support* and *Service Delivery*. These books describe the key processes an IT organization must employ in order to provide quality services to their customers.

The book *Service Support* reviews operational processes, like:

- Service Desk
- Incident Management
- Problem Management
- Change Management
- Release Management
- Configuration Management

ITIL's *Service Delivery* book covers tactical processes, including:

- Availability Management
- Capacity Management
- IT Service Continuity Management
- Service Level Management
- Financial Management for IT Services

The other six books in the ITIL library are:

- *Planning to Implement Service Management*
- *Application Management*

- *ICT Infrastructure Management*
- *Security Management*
- *Software Asset Management*
- *The Business Perspective: The IS View on Delivering Services to the Business.*[5] This is one of the true jewels of the ITIL library, and unfortunately often overlooked.

ITIL also provides three levels of training and certification:

- *Foundations Certificate,* a basic program useful to any IT professional, particularly those who want to understand the vocabulary of ITIL
- *Practitioner's Certificate,* helpful if you are going to specialize in one or more areas of ITIL
- *Manager's Certificate,* a more intensive program, best taken after a few years of foundation-level experience

ITIL certification is available from two companies who have been approved by the two official certifying agencies:

- ISEB[6] (Information Systems Exam Board), based in the United Kingdom
- EXIN[7] (Examination Institute for Information Science), based in the Netherlands

ITIL Terminology

Many organizations are standardizing on ITIL terminology, and for good reason. It removes many of the stumbling blocks to clear, efficient communication. For example, ITIL distinguishes between *customers* and *users*. *Customers* are the people within an organization who commission and fund IT services (generally senior managers). *Users* are the ones who consume these services on a day-to-day basis.

Here's another benefit of standardizing terminology. Three common terms often mean different things to different people: *incident, problem* and *error.* Adopting ITIL terminology reduces the confusion.

As we discussed earlier, in ITIL parlance, an *incident* is an event that is not part of the standard operation of service, which causes an interruption or reduction in the quality of that service. A *problem*, on the other hand, is an unknown underlying cause of one or more incidents. (One problem can trigger multiple incidents.) Once a problem's root cause has been identified, and a workaround or permanent solution developed, it is referred to as an *error*.

There have been extensions to ITIL, most notably the Microsoft Operations Framework (MOF) and the HP IT Service Management Reference Model.

Much of the ITIL framework is common sense, but it has the advantage of being fairly well documented. It's not necessary to jump full scale into ITIL implementation. You can easily embrace only the parts of it that make the most sense for your organization.

Things like change management and a configuration database are typically poorly implemented, and cost companies a lot of money. ITIL can help them go more smoothly.

As mentioned earlier, ITIL is not prescriptive. To help bridge the gap between theory and practice, HDI has published a book called *Implementing Service and Support Management Processes: A Practical Guide.*[8] It was developed for service and support managers as a reference to setting up and evolving current support center organizations, the book provides prescriptive guidance to implementing ITIL processes and other support center processes not in ITIL, and provides a focus on operational metrics for the support center.

Standard: Six Sigma

Six Sigma[9] is a quality measure and improvement program with its roots in manufacturing. It focuses on the control of a process to the point of $\pm$ six standard deviations (sigma) from a centerline – the equivalent of 3.4 defects per million. When one of your company's processes operates at Six Sigma, variations are so small that the resulting products or services are 99.9997% defect free.

The basic premise behind Six Sigma is the determination that data analysis drives business decisions, and root cause analysis drives implementation of solutions. Six Sigma is all about quality.

Six Sigma was first developed at Motorola, refined at AlliedSignal, and transformed into legend at GE under CEO Jack Welch. Since then it has attracted legions of new converts in myriad business sectors, including the service sector. The Six Sigma quality initiative has branched out from just manufacturing to a variety of service industries, including outsourcing, financial services and telecommunications organizations.

It may seem strange that a system with its roots in manufacturing can drive up the quality of services, particularly customer support. Many service companies don't think Six Sigma applies to them because people are at the heart of most service interactions. Another common reason is that many in the services business are uncomfortable with the heavy reliance on statistical data. Yet many companies have found that Six Sigma can help with process improvements of the services they offer.

Six Sigma shows that analyzing data and looking at root causes can uncover and implement solutions that improve even customer service interactions. For example, examining your company's billing procedures under the Six Sigma microscope could result in revamping the entire process to reduce billing discrepancies for the customer, reducing the number of service and complaint calls, thus improving the company's financial performance at the same time.

If your company utilizes Six Sigma, or is considering it, you should get involved early. Suspend your disbelief that it is only useful for manufacturing environments.

Best Practice: Knowledge Centered Support

Knowledge Centered Support,[10] formerly known as Solution Centered Support, is an emerging best practice in knowledge management for service and support organizations.

Created by the non-profit Consortium for Service Innovation, KCS defines a set of principles and practices that enable organizations to improve service levels to customers, gain operational efficiencies, and increase the organization's value to their company. The goal of KCS processes is to create and evolve findable and usable solutions.

KCS focuses on two parallel processes or loops. The *Solve* loop represents the individual workflow during the problem solving process. The *Evolve* loop is the quality improvement process that integrates the individual-level work with the organizational-level activities to improve the system (including the individual's ability.) Another way to think of the KCS double-loop process is that the *Solve* loop captures information, while the *Evolve* loop drives the organization's internal improvement.

For example, during a KCS *Solve* loop, the support person conversing with the customer captures relevant information during the process of delivering support. As she talks with the customer, she searches for existing knowledge by capturing the customer's situation in his own words.

If a solution isn't found in the organization's knowledge base, the information the customer has just provided becomes the basis of a new solution. But rather than collecting the information in a free-flow form, the support person captures the fix or workaround in a structured, actionable form. That way, the incident's solution can immediately be reused, even before it has been fully resolved. In this way, even before the incident has been resolved, its solution can be shared with other customer support team members.

Under KCS, anyone who is responsible for providing support can also create knowledge and add to the knowledge base. This is a departure from some organizations, where only a dedicated team is allowed to create knowledge. To ensure quality, KCS suggests that KCS champions and coaches review material from less experienced knowledge contributors to ensure it is accurate and timely.

The goal of KCS is to solve a problem once – and use the solution often. Greg Oxton, Executive Director of the Consortium for Service Innovation, the creators of KCS, says a staggering 60 to 90% of support requests *have already been dealt with before.* Ignoring all that accumulated knowledge, and concocting a new solution for each customer service call, is a phenomenal waste of time, effort and energy!

The most common customer service complaint is slow response time. According to a 2003 Service & Support Professionals Association study, 71% of customers griped about the length of time it took to resolve their issue. During an average 12 minute support call, the study revealed, support engineers spend as much as 70% of their time in problem diagnosis and knowledge search, but only 30% in problem resolution.

This might make sense when you are in your doctor's examining room. You probably want her to spend as much time as she needs figuring out exactly what's wrong with you – rather than quickly prescribing a fix for an ailment that's not bothering you.

As complicated as technical support can be, it's nowhere near as the complex as the human body. The trusty 80/20 rule suggests that 80% of all complaints can be resolved using only about 20% of an organization's knowledge. So it really shouldn't take that long to isolate the root cause of a problem. There is a fairly narrow range of issues that could be wrong. Of course, this is less true as you get into really complex support. For example, the root cause could be in the customer's environment, in your product or service, or in between, in something that neither of you has control of – the Internet.

KCS requires a shift in an organization's culture. Teamwork must be taken to a new level. At this higher level, knowledge is an asset, owned and maintained by a team – not by any one individual. No "heroes" needed!

KCS developed partly from the realization that the old-style linear thinking used in manufacturing does not necessarily map well to a knowledge-based company. As companies transcend feature-functionality and embrace relationship, loyalty and influence, some old business practices have become dysfunctional.

Embracing KCS can help reposition support executives. Instead of being perceived as merely implementing previously known solutions, their new role is creating connection and relevance inside their organizations on behalf of customers.

Methodology: Balanced Scorecard

After you have implemented one or more of these standards, frameworks and/or best practices, how do you measure and report the results? How do you communicate it to the rest of your organization? In the early 1990s, Drs. Robert Kaplan and David Norton created a management system they called the "Balanced Scorecard."

Essentially, the Balanced Scorecard[11] translates strategic vision into measurable performance indicators based on four perspectives:

- *Customer Perspective*. To achieve our strategic vision, how must we appear to customers?
- *Financial Perspective*. To succeed financially, how should we appear to our shareholders?
- *Internal Business Process Perspective*. To satisfy our shareholders and customers, what business processes must we excel at?
- *Learning and Growth Perspective*. To achieve our vision, how will we sustain our ability to change and improve?

The Balanced Scorecard is a method of designing, organizing and communicating performance measures across these four perspectives, using both short- and long-term time horizons. The scorecard conveys your organization's strategic plan to members. At the same time, it monitors all four perspectives simultaneously so that each continuously supports the strategic plan. The Balanced Scorecard is useful to help you see metrics in the context of the broad business perspective.

In my opinion, there are two interesting takeaways from adopting a balanced scorecard approach. One is that the balanced scorecard approach helps you and your team understand the big picture.

The other interesting takeaway from the Balanced Scorecard approach is that it helps you focus on those key metrics that are relevant to the entire business, not just those that are relevant to your part of it. For example, while ASA (Average Speed of Answer) may be a key metric for you, without context, it is meaningless to the rest of the company.

Tying It All Together

Now that we've reviewed a variety of best practices, frameworks, methodologies and standards, is there a way to tie them all together? So far, there isn't an accepted process for implementing and integrating all these different approaches.

Before starting any process improvement phase or framework, it is critical to take a detailed look at all the processes you currently use. Make sure you review them all. Remember: Just because you don't have *documented* processes does not mean that you don't have processes. Look for the undocumented ones, too.

For many businesses, particularly public companies, there are best practices or governances you must live by. Some are required by law; others are best practices in your profession. In fact, just about every department in your company may be guided by one or more of them.

Next, reach out to your colleagues in other departments and find out what best practices, standards and processes exist in their fields. Finally, try to tie various frameworks and methodologies together.

Note: If you want to know more about each framework or methodology turn back to the details of each one first, then come back to this overview.

The following graphic illustrates one possible way to think about tying together various frameworks, best practices and processes.

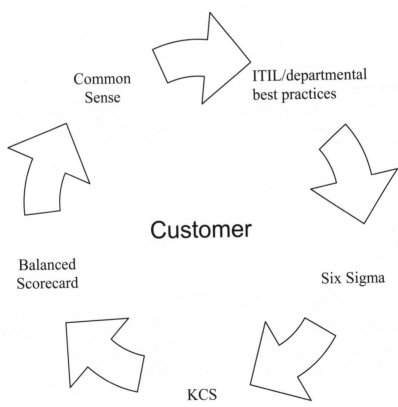

Common
Sense

ITIL/departmental
best practices

Customer

Balanced
Scorecard

Six Sigma

KCS

In terms of IT governance, ITIL is a good framework to start with. It's not perfect, but it's useful, particularly if your organization does not have formal processes or wants to see how you compare to what many consider IT's best practices.

Once you have your processes in place, how do you improve them? Six Sigma can help. While many Six Sigma projects begin with no data, if you have existing data and processes to build on, you have a head start. As noted earlier, Six Sigma, which started in the field of manufacturing, has been successfully adapted to the process tasks within a support organization.

You can create a learning organization using the best practices of KCS. They will help you capture the knowledge needed for an agile, customer-centric organization.

To keep things in perspective, there's the Balanced Scorecard. The fact is, most service organizations track a lot of things that make sense in terms of running their department, but don't mean much to the rest of the company or your customer. One way to take a more holistic view of service is to use the balanced scorecard approach and create reports and management dashboards based on that.

Finally, don't forget to use common sense. Don't blindly follow what others do. Ensure it will work in your organization and within your culture. Finally be sure to look at everything from your customer's perspective.

Don't Let Your Strengths Become Your Weaknesses

In Chapter 5, titled *People,* we introduced the idea of getting comfortable with being uncomfortable, and why you should re-examine your internal processes even when they appear to be working just fine.

This section examines an even more difficult problem to spot and fix – a strength that has become a weakness. After all, why fix something that is perceived to be a strength?

In your organization, there are probably a number of things you are proud of. Maybe they're attitudes, behaviors or services that your customers really like, and which set you apart from your competition.

But beware. The strengths that got you where you are today could become your Achilles heel tomorrow. It's easy to become so enamored of what has always worked (particularly when it becomes part of your corporate culture) that you fail to notice that your customer base or market conditions may have changed.

As an Ultimate Customer Support Executive, you should re-evaluate all service "truisms" in your company once a year.

During my years at Akamai, for example, we prided ourselves on being exceptionally customer-focused. Because of the very tight integration between external customer support and Engineering/QA, when a customer reported an issue, we could often isolate it, develop a workaround and deploy a patch or a fix to our 14,000 servers around the world – all within 24 hours! (Yes, the company did create some new processes to help ensure we stayed nimble.)

This quick response speed was necessary. After all, we were dealing with young, fast-growing companies like Yahoo! who were accustomed to moving at cyberspeed. Our speed was also a genuine service differentiator for us.

But as time went on, Akamai began working with larger and larger enterprises. With them, our rapid pace was perceived to be a liability. These giant customers were accustomed to waiting months, not hours, for their own organizations to issue bug fixes or patches. Our speedy response time made them skeptical. They assumed either we had known ahead of time that there was a problem and released the software anyway, or else we hadn't properly tested the software in advance.

Until we established trust with them, and showed them some of the innovative ways we developed to test and rapidly deploy software, it's no wonder some of these enterprises were skeptical. Considering their past experiences – how long other teams took to resolve issues and release fixes – no wonder they felt there was no other way we could possibly resolve their problems so quickly.

7 Technology

Any sufficiently advanced technology is indistinguishable from magic.

– Arthur C. Clarke, author

This chapter provides a high-level overview of some of the technologies available to the customer support organization. It's not an in-depth look, however. Technologies change so quickly that anything I discuss might be obsolete by the time you read this. A number of excellent online references and books are available that will walk you through specific tools and what they do. One such free online tool is the Phil Verghis' Help Desk FAQ[1] which has a comprehensive listing of tools and products available.

Most of us involved with technology tend to believe that customer support perfection is just one new technology away. By far the single most common mistake companies make is getting fixated on technology before optimizing their people and processes. Automating a mess only makes it messier, faster!

In 1994, during a Special Interest Group (SIG) at a support conference, I asked about 250 attendees how many were looking at getting a Customer Relationship Management (CRM) tool. About 100 raised their hands. When I asked how many were looking at their *second* CRM tool, about 90 of the 100 raised their hands. I would hazard a professional guess that in almost all those cases, their problem would not be fixed by replacing their existing tool. Only after you have hired the right people and implemented the right customer-centric processes does it make sense to look at automating.

But technology is essential for excellent customer service, isn't it? Most of us would agree. But before we examine some powerful technology tools, let's take a look at what is possible with the lowest of low tech tools. For a completely contrarian view, consider the *dabbawallahs*[2] of Mumbai, India.

First, a little background. Foods in India vary quite a bit, depending on the region where you live, the religion you practice and even within each family. For dietary and religious reasons, people are very particular about the type of food they eat. In addition, people in India generally prefer home-cooked meals to eating in a restaurant, and eating out is considerably more expensive than eating at home. Microwave ovens are not common in the workplace, and Indian food is traditionally eaten freshly prepared, not reheated. So taking lunch to work with you is a challenge. Not only are there many different dishes, it's difficult to keep foods hot, and with India's crowded public transportation, it can get quite messy if something spills.

So how do you get a hot, home cooked meal to work? Enter the 4,000 *dabbawallahs* of Mumbai, a city of about 15 million people. Their delivery business began in 1890. Originally all came from the same general region of India.

Here's how it works.

Every workday between 9 and 10 am, a *dabbawallah* stops by your home and picks up your *dabba*, the box of food you've prepared. Each *dabba* is fitted one above the other, and put into an outer tin case, which keeps the food warm and prevents it from spilling out. During rush hour, the *dabbawallah* picks up about 30 boxes, dodging rush-hour traffic on his bicycle, and delivers them to a waiting colleague at a pre-designated railway station. The boxes are sorted by destination, and another *dabbawallah* boards the train and escorts each set of boxes to the appropriate station.

At each station, teams re-sort thousands of *dabbas* by destination. Your *dabba*, and dozens of others, are handed off to yet another *dabbawallah*, who hops on his bicycle or pushcart, piled impossibly high with boxes, and delivers it to your office by noon. Whew! After lunch, the process is reversed, and the boxes return home before you do.

The cost? Less than US $10 a month. Each *dabbawallah* earns about US $100 a month.

Using this low-tech system, *dabbawallahs* manage to serve about 160,000 lunches a day, with the help of an army of workers, bicycles, push carts and the very crowded public train system in Mumbai. They are organized in teams of 20–25, and each team services a particular group of customers. Customer service is taken quite seriously. In fact, if there are 20 complaints, the entire team gets replaced.

Dabbawallahs don't have computers, most are functionally illiterate, and they are paid very low wages. In spite of all this, they achieve a quality rating of Six Sigma – on a par with that of Motorola!

The president of the Mumbai Tiffin Box Suppliers' Association said, "We do not have any technical support or corporate strategy. We consider our brain to be the computer which rarely commits an error."

He goes on to say, "We do not understand anything about Six Sigma rating. We simply do our work with dedication and find satisfaction in serving food to people, which in turn helps us make a living."

As you can tell, even in today's age of web-enabled generated real time tracking systems, a low-tech, people-intensive and process-intensive system can still work wonders.

Common Tools

Let's briefly review some of the technological tools available to customer support teams. Then we'll take a closer look at each.

- *Automatic Call Distribution* (ACD) systems distribute calls intelligently.
- *Interactive Voice Response* (IVR) units answer repetitive questions.

- *Workforce scheduling tools* help you decide how many people you need at work at any given time.
- *Issue tracking tools* or more comprehensive *Customer Relationship Management* tools help manage a customer's interactions with the company.
- *Self-service* tools enable a customer to help themselves, e.g., Knowledge Bases.

Other less common (but no less powerful) tools include:

- *Instant Messaging* (IM) systems enable real time communication between people.
- *Peer support* enable customers to help each other, often with little involvement from support staff.

If you think you don't have the resources or expertise to utilize these tools, don't despair! There are hosted models for all these tools that allow you to get started fairly inexpensively. For example, instead of upgrading your phone switches and internal hardware and software to handle Voice over IP (VoIP) telephony, you can have a third party handle it in a fraction of the time it would take to install it yourself.

Automatic Call Distribution (ACD)

An Automatic Call Distribution (ACD) system helps you manage customer phone calls more efficiently. The best way to explain what an ACD does is to look at what happens without one. Let's say you have a staff of ten people handling incoming phone queries from customers. Without an ACD, when the phone rings, all ten extensions ring at once.

Inevitably, your most conscientious staff members pick up the phone as quickly as possible. If you only focus on the "average speed of answer" (how long it took, on average, to answer each incoming call) all looks well.

But look closely at your phone statistics and you'll find uneven work distribution. Some of your employees will not be pulling their weight. They will assume that someone else will get the phone first, so they're in no big rush to pick up. This may not even be malicious. They might assume that what they are working on is more important at that moment.

This situation is a recipe for morale problems. Eventually your most productive phone agents will become unhappy about the uneven workload.

Now let's see what happens with an ACD system. Instead of the phone ringing simultaneously on everyone's desk, you can choose from an array of configurations. One solution is a "round robin" of calls, where a call rings at each individual extension in a predetermined order. Or you can route the next incoming call to the person who has been off the phone the longest, or to the person who has the best skills to handle the call.

With skills-based routing, each call goes to the person with a specific skill set. For example, your department might have two teams of people with specialized computing expertise. One team knows Linux well, let's say, and the other can knows Windows XP well. An ACD system lets you create sets of "rules" that determine how calls are handled. When a call comes in and the caller indicates they have a Linux question, a "rule" can ensure that the call is routed to one of the Linux specialists. A second rule could specify that the Linux specialist who has been off the phone the longest gets the next call for Linux support. As you can imagine, ACDs offer a lot of features at a considerable range of prices.

Automatic Call Distribution systems also assist with disaster recovery plans. They allow you to have certain sites back up each other in different time zones. If, say, your Atlanta support center is offline because of an ice storm, an ACD can automatically divert all calls to your London facility.

Note: Voice Over IP (VoIP) systems, which route telephone calls over the Internet, can dramatically lower long distance costs and provide additional capabilities.

Staff members can work from home, for example, with all the functionality they'd have if they were in the office.

If your organization doesn't currently have an ACD, I'd strongly recommend that you consider getting one. Even in small organizations, it is quite possible that other departments or groups need the kind of features an ACD offers. Talk to your peers and see if you can join forces with other departments for a more sophisticated system than your department might have been able to afford on its own.

For example, when I was at Duke University, the Office of Information Technology had too small a staff to justify a high end ACD or workforce scheduling program. We reached out to the Duke University Medical Center (a completely autonomous group) and shared a common ACD system. This provided both groups with better tools than either of us could have afforded on our own, and gave our customers a more seamless experience.

Interactive Voice Response Units (IVR)

IVRs are the link between your computer databases and customers calling for service and support. They allow callers to speak in their natural voice to complete transactions or queries over the phone.

Interactive Voice Response units can be used quite successfully in high volume call centers, particularly with repetitive queries like internal or external directory assistance, order confirmation and a multitude of self-service options. IVRs can increase your support staff's productivity and job satisfaction, because they'll spend less time responding to routine questions and more time focusing on delivering quality service.

IVRs are most effective in well-structured interactions where the subject matter is known in advance. Answers are pre-recorded and typically specified by a "tree" menu such as "Welcome to the XYZ Company. Please say one of the following choices…"

Warning: If not implemented properly, IVRs can be really painful for the customer. Just ask anyone who has been stuck in an endless loop, trapped in the dreaded "voice mail jail."

Workforce Scheduling Tool

A workforce scheduling tool uses existing incoming calling patterns to predict what kind of staffing you'll need in the future. Based on statistical models, these tools create work schedules that also take into account any business rules you specify.

A workforce scheduling tool can help you answer the following types of questions:

- What kind of service will your customers experience?
- How many agents do you need to support a given call volume?
- What percentage of their time will your staff spend answering calls?
- How many callers will hang up before receiving service?

If you want only a rough idea how many staff you need at any one time, you can get by with an inexpensive (or free) Erlang-based calculator that you can find on the Internet or in my free Help Desk FAQ, listed in the Appendix. These calculators can determine how many people you'll need at any given time, but typically won't actually create a work schedule for your staff. You'll have to do this manually.

A full-fledged workforce scheduling tool does much more than these simple calculators. For example, how many people do you need for "off phone" work, such as meetings, outgoing phone calls, email handling, breaks and time off, etc.? You can get a rough idea by adding this time to the call handling time. This lets you roughly approximate the workload even for non-phone work. In many centers, however, workers neglect to track all the outgoing phone calls they make while resolving a customer's issue. They count only incoming calls as workload. This is a mistake that a workforce scheduling tool can fix.

In a university setting, for example, the percentage of outgoing queries to incoming queries can be 30–40%, a non-trivial amount of work that is often not considered when looking at straightforward metrics.

More advanced workforce scheduling tools go beyond simply letting you know how many people you need. They allow staff to self-select shifts (based on your guidelines), without your intervention.

> *Example*: Suppose that two staff members – Sheila and Susan – both want New Year's Day off. Based on historical call volumes and types of calls, the workforce scheduling tool sees that one or the other will be needed that day. If your business rules state that the person with most seniority gets first preference for time off, the tool will take that into consideration. In this case, it automatically notifies Susan that she can have New Year's Day off. It also notifies Sheila that she will have to work.

In general, workforce scheduling tools give you a good handle on the staffing levels you need. They can also provide background data for staffing discussions based on company-defined levels of service.

Trouble Ticket/Customer Relationship Management Systems

In the early days, a customer support flowchart looked a lot like the ones used by nurses. Like nurses, customer service personnel logged complaints (symptoms) reported by customers (patients). In fact, the earliest versions of customer support documents compared a "trouble ticket" to a patient's hospital chart. Both sought to define a problem and coordinate the efforts of several different people, who would work on the different parts of the problem at different times.

Another clue of how much technical support has borrowed from nursing is the word *triage*, still used by some organizations to describe their front line support. On the battlefield, triage is the process of quickly evaluating mass casualties and assigning priorities for treatment. Typically, the wounded were sorted into three groups:

- Those needing immediate treatment
- Those whose wounds could wait a little while for treatment, and
- Those who were expected to die

The rationale behind triage was simple. In an emergency situation, you cannot waste resources on those who are likely to die anyway.

While there may be a place for triage in some support situations, I shudder when I hear the term used on a day-to-day basis. It implies that your support team is operating in crisis mode – which suggests that your customers are already in serious pain. Ultimately, of course, that means your company will be, too.

Even the term "trouble ticket" is inappropriate. Do you perceive customers calling for service and support as trouble? If so, you'd better change your attitude. Your competitors would no doubt welcome a chance for that kind of trouble.

Today, trouble ticketing systems are more commonly called issue tracking systems, or are part of more comprehensive Customer Relationship Management (CRM) systems. A CRM system allows you to maintain customer and/or employee profiles, log problems or "incidents," provide work queues to organize, prioritize, manage and route work, while allowing for escalations and business rules. Many allow you to automate change management processes. These ensure standardized methods and techniques for efficient and prompt handling of all changes, and prevent incidents that are related to unanticipated consequences of changes.

The idea behind a CRM system is to have the same information available to everyone in the company, so every product or service need of the customer is met. It is increasingly common for a customer to telephone you to follow up an email they sent, about an order they had placed online last week. A CRM system can integrate all these disparate channels of interaction, and give you a holistic picture of all the customer's interactions with your company. Many can manage outbound communications with customers as well.

A CRM system is invaluable in really understanding your customer base. For example, it is much easier to determine if a customer is truly profitable (as opposed to merely bringing in a lot of revenue) when all interactions with the customer are captured in a CRM tool, and then that information is matched against financial information.

CRM tools may sound like the ideal solution to your problems. But, as always, the quality of what you get out of the system is no better than what you put into it, and how you designed it. Often data is polluted or incomplete, and improper decisions are based on bad data. Many smaller customer support groups will find standalone issue tracking systems will suit their needs just fine. However, if you are part of a larger organization, and want to get a holistic view of your customer, you should consider a CRM system.

Numerous issue tracking/CRM tools are available, with prices ranging from freeware to multi-million dollar implementations.

Self-Service Tools/Knowledge Bases

Self-service refers to customers getting the assistance they need without contacting a support person. For our purposes, this includes information on documentation, software updates, entering and viewing incidents, training, diagnostic tools, knowledge bases, etc.

Customers generally decide for themselves when to use self-service tools and when they feel they need to speak to a "live" human being. In general, when a customer thinks he can get the solution more quickly himself, he will choose self-service. The more critical or time-sensitive the issue, the more likely he is to seek out a human being. Thus, routine transactions like software documentation and updates are great candidates for self-service.

Implementing self-service tools is quite compelling from a financial point of view. Studies show the cost of speaking to a support person by phone ranges from a low of $7 (for a first-tier support person) to as much as $70 per call (for highly technical support staff). By contrast, most self-service support can be provided for as little as 5–10% of that cost.

Because of the dramatic savings, many companies see self-service tools solely as a mechanism to reduce costs, rather than a way for customers to resolve their issues more quickly and efficiently.

Worse, some companies encourage their customers to use electronic forms of communication – then punish them for complying. For example, many companies have targets for how quickly their customer service people answer the phone – say, within 60 seconds. But their guideline for answering an email is usually one business day. That's 1,440 times slower! If you want to encourage people to contact you via email, why force them to wait longer when they do?

Here are suggested best practices for making the most of your self-service site:

- *Update your website frequently.* Fresh content is compelling. A stale support site is not much use. Many companies have found that customers visit their support sites periodically, even when they don't have a problem. This makes sense. If your website is packed with new, useful content, people will keep coming back and learning new things each time.

- *Double-check the usability* of your website offerings. You may think it's easy to navigate and use, but have you asked your customers what they think? Focus groups are one way to uncover useful information about your support website.
- *Actively promote your support website.* Some customers may not be aware it even exists, so remind them at every opportunity. Make sure your entire customer-facing team includes a reference to it in their email signatures.
- *Offer liberal incentives* to your customers and partners for using your self-service tools. Some companies, like Mercury Interactive, even give points for usage that can be redeemed for goodies.
- *Staff it appropriately.* You cannot just hope that someone will keep your support website up to date. You cannot "force fill" it either. This is the well-intentioned but ineffective practice of requiring your team to add a pre-determined number of knowledge-based entries per month. Almost invariably this approach eventually leads to garbage over time.

There is a new self-service support metric called *deflection* – i.e., contact avoidance. It refers to a customer seeking help via the web who does not call you later – suggesting she found what she needed. Like many other metrics in self-service, deflection is not an easily quantifiable number. That does not mean it should not be measured, only that we need better language to describe new activities.

One way to measure deflection is to keep track of how many people contact you within 24 hours of searching your knowledge base or other self-service tools on the same subject. This is a rough proxy to measure the usage and effectiveness of your self-service tools.

An investment in self-service technologies can make a big difference in cost and customer satisfaction.

Example: In 1996, Internet usage was taking off in a big way at many universities in the United States. When I worked at Duke University's Office of Information Technology, as I mentioned before, one perennial issue was managing the huge number of calls during the back to school rush each September. In 1997, we launched a website with answers to frequently asked questions (FAQs). That was a dramatic success, as the following statistics show.

During the September crunch in 1996, the OIT Help Desk received 17,500 direct inquiries (primarily by e-mail and phone) and 7,200 hits to the Help Desk website, totaling 24,700 hits. The next year, after posting the FAQs on our website, the total number of inquiries more than doubled to 53,200. Yet the number of direct inquiries rose only slightly, to 18,200. At the same time, web inquiries rose dramatically to 35,000.

When you offer more opportunities for customers to help themselves, you may also find the characteristics of incoming queries changes. For example, the average call length (or contact length) may actually *increase,* since most of the simple questions are now being handled by the customers themselves.

Self-Healing Technology

Most companies are fixated on *good* service, i.e., service after the customer has noticed an issue and contacted them about it. Very few companies make the leap to great service – taking care of issues even before they impact the customer.

This is where self-healing technologies come in. For technology providers, self-healing technologies can lift service and support to the next level. These technologies can automatically identify and resolve certain types of problems before the customer even notices, reducing or eliminating the need for service calls. This is accomplished by embedding systems with diagnostic tools that trap an issue and alert customer support when something is wrong.

Example: Suppose hard-drive space is running low. Self-healing tools can be configured to notice and send alerts to both the customer and customer support. Customer support can then make a proactive, courtesy call to the customer to alert them of the issue, before it has a chance to deteriorate into a serious problem.

Other examples of these self-healing tools include software that takes snapshots of your customer's computer environment, allowing you to roll back changes that might cause system instability.

Think of these self-healing tools as layers of defenses. Probably no single layer is enough to protect you from serious problems. But working together, they should prevent enough problems, and deflect enough incoming customer service contacts, to make a difference in the operations of your support team.

IBM, Sun and HP have spent millions on self-optimizing, self-diagnostic, and self-healing systems. IBM calls their initiative "Autonomic Computing," HP labels theirs the "Adaptive Enterprise," and Sun's version is named "N1 Initiative." All of them seek to reduce the complexity of managing computer systems, and shrink the vast amounts of money spent by corporations around the world in managing technology.

Instant Messaging (IM)

Instant messaging is second nature to most young people with access to technology. Young people, especially those under the age of 20, use IM to chat with friends. They're so adept at using it, they think nothing of carrying on separate, simultaneous conversations with ten or more friends, each in their own tiny window.

In corporations, IM is not as popular. There are three primary reasons for this. Historically, instant messaging was not secure enough to satisfy IT departments. Nor was it easy to retain permanent archives or an audit trail of instant messages, which might be required during a legal proceeding. Finally, there were no administrative tools good enough to manage hundreds or even thousands of accounts.

All these drawbacks are increasingly being addressed, and it is well worth looking at IM. It can be a very powerful tool to add to an enterprise's support toolkit.

> *My take:* No matter what your official stance is on IM, if you audit the tools currently in use in your corporation, you will probably find that instant messaging has spread all over, much the way PCs sneaked in during the reign of the mainframe. IM is here. Get over it and embrace it!

Incorporating IM into your support toolkit offers one distinct advantage: speed. Internal support teams can collaborate and coordinate much more quickly using IM than with traditional channels, especially when addressing fast-moving situations. For example, if a team member is struggling with a particularly tough question, she can instantly query other support staffers for assistance on the solution (after she has checked the self-service knowledge base, of course). This allows her to gather and deliver possible solutions in real time, while the customer is still on the phone.

Peer Support

Peer support refers to customers helping each other when they need assistance. This makes the most sense in complex technical support environments, particularly when your customers can build on or modify your product. Peer support embodies the principle that your customers may know as much or more about your products than you do. After all, they are using them in many different ways, limited only by their imaginations.

Peer support can resolve many customer questions without the involvement of your support staff. A well-run peer support community can create an army of volunteer experts. They can add big value at minimal cost, via knowledge creation as well as product improvement.

This approach lets you leverage your organization's "power users." As in most human endeavors, a small percentage of the participants contribute the most. This suggests you are probably best off cultivating a small, core group of power users.

> *For example:* Novell has long been a leader in the use of peer support. They have 5 full-time staff members dedicated to helping a small cadre of 35 power users. These 35 power users, in turn, form the vanguard of a team that supports tens of thousands of users.

Effective peer support systems are based on rewarding the few power users who are support superstars. The elite are recognized and rewarded for being the best of the best and for helping so many other customers.

But there is one potential flaw in this, and it is rooted in cultural differences. In many societies, standing out is not good. You are seen as a nail that needs to be hammered in, to become more like everyone else. This attitude is particularly true in non-individualistic societies, those that score low on Hofstede's Individualism scale, which is discussed in the next chapter. Indeed, if you examine your peer support superstars, you will find that most are either from Western societies, or have spent significant amounts of time in or working with the West.

The challenge for vendors is to better understand how to encourage the rest of the world to become power users. It may be as simple as changing the nature of the reward. Try making your rewards team-oriented, as opposed to rewarding an individual.

8 Global Support

Don't worry about the world coming to an end today. It's already tomorrow in Australia.

— Charles M. Schulz, cartoonist

Let's face it. It can be pretty intimidating to start working with people around the world, much less catering to their needs, or managing them, or being managed by them. Many business etiquette books contain useful advice. For example, in Japan, you're advised to exchange business cards with both hands. When receiving a business card, you're supposed to examine both sides carefully. Do not immediately put it away. While this is all useful information, it does not help you better manage an employee or better serve a customer.

This chapter has information on understanding different cultures and managing global support operations.

Cultural Primers

Do human beings, deep down inside, possess basic beliefs and norms that are universally valid? Many of us who live in, or are influenced by, Western society feel they do. Unfortunately, it's not true. Experts call this mistaken assumption "universalism," and it can cause serious misunderstandings when dealing with people from different cultural backgrounds or with different beliefs.

Fortunately, many excellent resources are available to help you better understand other societies, and how their people think and behave. One such resource is Professor Geert Hofstede's website, *Cultural Dimensions*.[1]

Hofstede, a professor at Maastricht University in The Netherlands, conducted perhaps the most comprehensive study of how values in the workplace are influenced by culture. His findings are useful in understanding both our staffs and our customers.

Hofstede analyzed a large database of employee values scores collected by IBM between 1967 and 1973. From the initial results and later additions, he identified four primary dimensions that differentiate the world's cultures. He called them *power distance*, *individualism*, *masculinity*, and *uncertainty avoidance*.

Later Hofstede added a fifth dimension – *long-term orientation*. The following definitions of each dimension are from his website.

- *Power Distance Index (PDI)* focuses on the degree of equality or inequality between people in each society.
- *Individualism* (IDV) focuses on the importance each society places on individual or collective achievement and interpersonal relationships.
- *Masculinity* (MAS) focuses on how much importance a society places on the traditional masculine work role model of male achievement, control, and power.
- *Uncertainty Avoidance Index* (UAI) focuses on each society's tolerance for uncertainty and ambiguity, i.e. unstructured situations.
- *Long-Term Orientation* (LTO) measures a society's long-term devotion to traditional, forward-thinking values.

Hofstede's research studied people from many different countries to see where they place along the five dimensions. For example, his research shows that India has a low Uncertainty Avoidance Index of 40, compared to the world average of 65. This means that as a culture, Indians are more open to unstructured ideas and situations. Contrast this with Mexico, which has a UAI of 82. This suggests that Mexican society has a very low tolerance for uncertainty. Perhaps recognizing its people's distaste for uncertainty, Mexico has adopted and implemented strict rules, laws, policies, and regulations.

Another useful resource for understanding other societies that I've enjoyed and learned a lot from is *Working Across Cultures,*[2] by John Hooker, a professor at Carnegie Mellon University in Pittsburgh, PA USA. Hooker approaches culture from a background in cultural anthropology, and his book addresses culture as it relates to space, time, and context. Hooker devotes several chapters to cultures in specific countries, including Mexico, Germany, Denmark, China, India, Zimbabwe and Turkey.

One interesting area that Hooker explores is the difference between "rules-based" and "relationship-based" cultures. In a rules-based culture, individual behavior is governed by rules. People comply mostly because of the guilt and fear they feel if they break a rule, even if no one observes the infraction. But in a relationship-based culture, individual behavior is governed by relationships between people.

How does all this relate to us? As you begin providing support to people in different countries, you may need to tailor your services and approach to each culture. As the old song goes, different strokes for different folks. You cannot apply the same policies and procedures everywhere and expect to get the same results.

> *For example:* In some relationship-based societies, people view rules, whether about support hours or stopping at a deserted stop sign, as mere guidelines that must be weighed in the context of the situation. When dealing with customers in these cultures, you will need to build in additional flexibility for each situation.

Understanding some of the other theories in Hooker's book – about "high context" and "low context" cultures, for example – can help you better understand why what works in one society may not work in another.

Northern European countries are low context societies, for example. Everything is spelled out clearly, and people respect what is written down. In these cultures, you'll find that a written notice informing people of a change in your support policies is noted and observed by most.

In contrast, high context cultures like India's are not used to reading signs to find out what to do. Instead, they get this information from friends, family and other people. In this kind of culture, a written notice informing people of a change in support hours may not even be noticed. To draw attention to those kinds of changes, you will need to find additional methods that match the culture of these societies.

Global Support Models

Global support is a luxury that only big corporations with deep pockets can afford, right? Wrong! The reality is, if you have an international customer base, you can no longer afford to keep doing business as usual. It's just not enough anymore.

As an Ultimate Customer Support Executive, you must look at the entire customer experience from the customer's point of view. This is particularly important when dealing with international customers.

There are a number of ways to configure customer service so that it takes good care of your international customers. The key is to create a balance between global consistency and local responsiveness. This balance is likely to change over time, by the way, and that is OK.

Let's look at some of the most common ways to handle global support.

Centralized Support Model

In this model, authority is concentrated in one location, usually with a support executive located at the company headquarters. There is a clear chain of command that flows up to a single individual who has ultimate accountability for all global support issues.

For very small support organizations, this could mean that worldwide support is handled by staff in just one country. There may not be support locations or support staff in any other parts of the world.

Larger support organizations generally have local support offices in several locations. For these organizations, a centralized support model typically means that local staff handles the relatively small number of calls coming in from their own geographic region, but does not provide after-hours support, which is handled by the headquarters support team.

If your remote support groups are large enough, centralized support usually morphs into a Follow the Sun or a Regional Hubs model, discussed below.

Centralized Support Pros

- *Centralized decision-making,* so there is less confusion over who does what.
- *Faster decision-making,* since there are far fewer negotiations between support leaders in different geographic regions.
- *A single set of tools* is typically used by everyone, which makes it easier for support people to maintain a holistic view of the customer.
- *Common support contracts and offerings,* which are better for customers.

Centralized Support Cons

- *Difficult to offer support customized for local needs,* both in terms of hours of coverage as well as languages offered. Support languages offered are typically limited to the languages spoken by support staff.

- *Can alienate customers or prospects* in areas where need for local support is acute due to cultural or linguistic requirements (e.g., Korea, Japan, France).

Follow the Sun Model

In this model, multiple support centers around the world coordinate service to provide business-hours support to their local customers, and off-hours support to the rest of the company's customers. This enables a company to provide live 24 x 7 support without requiring any one location to be staffed 24 x 7.

Here's a typical example. A US East Coast office answers calls during its workday, and provides off-hours support to other regions whose offices are closed. When the East Coast staff goes home for the night, the US West Coast office takes over. Later, the Indian office takes over from the US West Coast office, and the European office picks up after the Indian office shuts down. Later, Europe hands off support responsibility back to the US East Coast office.

While this model might seem complicated, it can actually be implemented without a large staff in each region. It does require tight integration between various back-office systems and highly coordinated processes to allow for a seamless interface handoff between different support groups.

This model typically works well when there is a strong executive with global responsibilities, i.e., a centralized support model.

If you have enough staff, a popular variation is "regional hubs." With this model, each regional hub acts like a local head office for support for that region, and gives regional customers the unique support they need. In this model, you might have pan-European support coming out of your Irish office, for example, and Far Eastern support out of Singapore or Australia. This model delivers economies of scale (enough support people for backup, training and learning) within a region.

Follow the Sun/Regional Hubs Pros

- *Off-hours support* is covered by an office that is already scheduled to work
- *Around the clock work on customer issues,* by handing them off between support teams
- *Staff works standard business hours,* rather than shifts
- *Standardized systems and processes*
- *Common tools* around the world
- *Consistent training* across the globe
- *Greater flexibility for local each unit* even with this standardization
- *Excellent for disaster recovery*

Follow the Sun/Regional Hubs Cons

- *More expensive to setup,* though VoIP systems are dramatically driving down costs
- *Difficult to convince local sales offices* to give up some of their local-only support for the greater good
- *Coordinating far-flung groups* can be complex
- *Requires strong leadership and trust* among different units
- *More than one staff member* is typically required at each location, otherwise shift coverage issues can result
- *Language skills need to be excellent,* particularly if people whose primary language is not English will be providing support to people in another region whose primary language is also not English

Decentralized Model

In the decentralized model, no one person or unit has ultimate authority over support decisions. Instead, authority is distributed among different support entities. This model of support often follows the corporate philosophy, and is often implemented after mergers and acquisitions. It is also common when the parent company has a decentralized model with independent business units, and each local unit runs as an independent operation.

In the decentralized model, support leadership in each country is usually provided by local sales executives, and often differs quite a bit among regions.

Decentralized Pros

- *Far more responsive* to local sales needs
- *Staff feels personally accountable* for success of their customers

Decentralized Cons

- *Potentially the most wasteful of support setups,* with duplication of tools, inconsistent procedures, etc.
- *Can be difficult for global customers* due to inconsistent support contracts, different escalation policies, etc.
- *Local offices often choose systems and policies* that make sense for them, but result in an overall sub-optimal experience for the customer
- *Training, if any, is done independently,* which can result in inconsistent customer experiences

Conclusion

In my opinion, support should be centrally managed, but locally distributed. This means one individual is accountable for global service and support, yet implementation is very receptive to local needs. In general, the model that best fits this description is the regional hubs model, but by no means is this the only "right" way to do it. If you choose this method, make sure that all regions and localities are given the chance to participate and share ideas.

Managing Support Centers Globally

Very often, people have managerial responsibilities for global support centers thrust on them with little background or training. If you find yourself in this situation, or if your formal training was a little less than complete, here are some tips that I've learned along the way.

Take Care of Yourself and Your Family

When you work with global support, you will be dealing with a 24-hour workday. Depending on your team's locations, you may have very early morning phone calls and very late night phone calls, punctuated by the normal busy day. You will have to take long business trips that disrupt your sleep patterns, endure jet lag, eat food that may not always agree with you, and generally do things that are outside your comfort zone. The work itself can be very satisfying and make a big difference to company and customer alike. However, if you are not careful, you and your family will suffer. Talk about your new, busier workload with your family ahead of time.

Every once in a while, unplug yourself from the potentially job- or family-crippling business of global support. Talk to others who have been in the same position, and get tips on how they coped. Don't forget to take care of yourself and your family while you handle this important responsibility.

Do Your Homework

The best way to begin is to learn more about the region you are supporting. Earlier in this chapter I recommended John Hooker's book and Geert Hofstede's website for a high-level understanding of the culture you are working with.

Take time to study the culture of the region where your support teams are based, and the culture of your customers. For example, in societies with a high Power Distance Index, people may not openly challenge their bosses. In this environment, people may be unwilling to disagree with you openly. They'll keep their opinions to themselves. When a staffer in this culture says "OK," it may only indicate that he heard you – not necessarily that he agrees with you.

Another good way to find out more about a country is to speak with a native. Perhaps someone in your organization is originally from that country. If so, seek them out. If you work in or near a university, contact its Office of International Students or a similar department to see if there is a professor or student from the region you are interested in. They will usually be glad to help you if you take the time to reach out and contact them.

These contacts may also help you pick up insider information, like which universities are highly rated (helpful as you evaluate hiring locals), reputable companies, local expectations for service, etc.

Face-to-Face Contact

In many parts of the world, nothing replaces a face-to-face meeting for showing a customer that you care about them. In relationship-based countries, in-person meetings are the building blocks on which business deals are made.

This emphasis on face-to-face contact is also true in high-wage Japan, says Tatsumi Yamashita, CEO and Founder of HDI Japan/ThinkService KK. He says that even in metropolitan Tokyo, with a population of 30 million people, dispatching people to see a customer after a problem is expected. Tatsumi-san says that face to face customer support generates the highest satisfaction in Japan.

Tatsumi-san says that a senior support engineer in Japan expects to visit 2-3 customers a day, to apologize in person after a customer impacting issue occurs.

Visit your team and customers at least once or twice a year, and budget for your team members to come and visit you once a year. When your team visits, make it a point to take them around to meet with all the other groups that they deal with, and introduce them in person. Make sure that their trip is productive and also fun.

Get Out!

I would strongly recommend that every Ultimate Customer Support Executive spend at least part of their career working in a remote office (i.e., far away from headquarters, where all the action typically is). Only then will you make the leap from theoretical understanding to a true grasp of the often lonely and confusing world of a remote worker.

One of the most serious issues faced by people working in remote sites is feeling isolated and ignored. This is even worse for support staff in other countries, since they are so dependent on getting the latest information and training in order to serve their customers. To make matters worse, sometimes they have to absorb that communication and deal with customers in a language that is not their primary language, struggling to extract what is meant from what is literally said.

This is even more difficult in high-context societies. Email and phone conversations are both bereft of non-verbal clues, so for members of these cultures they are not easy methods of communication.

Get out there and experience some of this isolation and disorientation yourself. It will push you to come up with truly innovative solutions of your own.

Acknowledge Cultural Pride

In many parts of the world, even less-developed regions, people resent having old technology dumped on them. They are brand conscious. They want the latest and greatest, not hand-me-downs. This means that the products and services you provide your team in those regions should be as good as your flagship versions back at headquarters.

Furthermore, don't assume that technological standards in remote areas are inferior to those in Western countries. Let's look at an example. Many IT departments have a standard for Internet connectivity at headquarters, and a different (usually lower) set of standards for smaller offices. This may not play well internationally.

Here's why. In Japan, customers can get souped-up DSL lines with blazing speeds of 24-26 Mbps for only about $30 a month. This is far faster than cable and DSL connections in the US and most other parts of the world, including many businesses. Your employees in Japan will not take lightly to having a slower connection at work than they have at home. How would you like it if your international global corporate parent mandated a 56K dial up connection as the only way to connect with the internet, even from your office?

Globalization and Localization

Being a global company today involves more than just selling your products or services around the world. It means that your products or services must be relevant to the local marketplace. This takes more than mere translation. The non-profit Localization Industry Standardization Association[3] (LISA) defines localization as "the process of modifying products or services to account for differences in distinct markets."

LISA identifies three main categories that localization should address: language, content and cultural, and technical issues. Let's look at them one at a time.

Language: Today, English is the closest thing to a universal language in the world of service and support. but don't assume that your customers speak and understand written English. They may, but they may not want to, or they may be uncomfortable with it.

You should at least provide accurate translations of your documentation for foreign customers. Recent advances in Globalization Management Systems (which are industry-specific versions of Content Management Systems) have made translations of complex websites and documents easier than ever before.

But be careful. Mistranslations, when they happen, can range from the funny to the disastrous. In the worst cases, they can even damage the brand. Perdue is a major brand of chicken in the US. Their slogan is, "It takes a strong man to make a tender chicken." But when translated into Spanish, it came out, "It takes an aroused man to make a chick affectionate." This unfortunate message was plastered on billboards all over Mexico.

Content and Cultural: Be aware that values can change across borders. In some countries, for example, time is not seen as something you can put a premium on. In these areas, if you're trying to package tiers of support, from the least expensive to the most costly, you may not have much luck trying to sell a premium support service that includes onsite visits to justify the higher price. In many countries, onsite visits may simply be expected as part of purchase price.

Another example: In many parts of India it is not uncommon for bankers to stop by your house to drop off and pick up paperwork, if it is inconvenient for you to visit the bank. This is not just for the wealthy.

Technical: Internationalization essentially consists of abstracting the functionality of a product away from any particular language. Doing this allows programmers to add specific language support back in, when it is time to localize the product to a particular language.

> *Tip:* The term "I18N" is often used in technical circles. It is shorthand for the word "internationalization," with the 18 representing the number of letters between the "I" and the "N."

Without I18N, all computer users would have to learn English before learning to use a computer, which would be a non-starter.

Ethics

Working with other cultures will quickly bring you face to face with the question of ethics. You'll quickly discover that what is considered "ethical" and "unethical" can change drastically in different places. What is considered immoral and corrupt in one country may be seen as perfectly acceptable and commonplace in another.

As you recall, in rules-based societies, people follow the rules. Guilt and fear force people to toe the line, even if no one is there to see them cross it. On the other hand, in relationship-based countries, there are fewer absolutes. Rules are often seen as mere guidelines, to be decided in the context of each individual situation.

This can lead to dilemmas for those of us doing business overseas. The Foreign Corrupt Practices Act of 1977 made it illegal for US companies to pay bribes overseas. In 1997, the 29 member nations of the Organization for Economic Cooperation and Development passed similar anti-corruption laws, bringing many European and Japanese companies under the same rules.

Nevertheless, if you deal with other entities, particularly in bureaucratic countries, you may be expected to "grease the wheels" with an illegal gratuity. How should you respond?

My advice: Stay away from bribes and anything unethical within the context of your own organization. Get guidance from your legal team and nationals in your company who hail from other countries. They can be a valuable resource to help navigate this ethical minefield.

Understand Legal Implications of Overseas Labor

When you start managing international teams of employees, you will learn a lot more about international law than you might have expected. Confer with your company's legal department to find out more about labor laws in other countries before you make any assumptions.

For example, suppose you want to make your French operation part of your global support team. Specifically, you want your support person there to start putting in some mandatory after-hours coverage. Let's assume that up to now, she was working only her regular work hours, with no mandatory after-hours work.

This involves a change in the employee's job classification, and is not a trivial process. In the United States, asking someone to change their job is relatively easy to do, provided they are properly compensated.

But overseas, very often you will have to deal with third parties to execute some portion of your international support. Be aware of the geographic and cultural differences with respect to contracts *before* you negotiate.

For example, in a rules-based culture, a contract is the end of negotiations. It is possible to negotiate with a complete stranger and come up with a binding contract a day later.

But in some relationship-based cultures – for example China, the very concept of a contract may be alien. If you are friends, then there is no need for a contract – a handshake will do. After all, in that culture, the relationship between the two parties is far more important than a contract. If you are not a friend – well, the contract is merely an understanding that you have agreed to work together. Don't be surprised if the real discussions begin *after* the contract has been signed!

Don't consider this unethical or immoral. It is just different from what you are used to. As an Ultimate Customer Support Executive, you should be aware of any cultural differences before you start negotiating, and be clear about the different sets of expectations you each bring to the table.

Interview: Tatsumi Yamashita

Tatsumi Yamashita is CEO and Founder of HDI Japan/ThinkService KK.

Q: What would a non-Japanese person find unique about providing technical support or customer service in Japan?

A: Japanese customers expect excellent customer service, with every service interaction. On the other hand, Japanese people don't like making a scene and many people don't complain about bad service. They just don't do business with companies that they don't get excellent service from.

Q: Can you offer any suggestions for a company that is trying to provide support to customers in Japan?

A: First, plan on learning Japanese. 98% of Japanese citizens communicate in Japanese only.

Use Japanese customer support personnel. Because we are an isolated island country, Japan has some unique customs. Customer support people should know the Japanese culture well. It will help a lot in providing excellent customer service.

Understand, the Japanese are predisposed toward big names, big brands. The Japanese economy is controlled by big companies. In fact, 80% of workers work for companies with more than 50 employees, a far larger proportion than in the United States. Many people believe that a big brand is reliable. This is also true for Western brands.

9 Offshoring

If the world operates as one big market, every employee will compete with every person anywhere in the world who is capable of doing the same job. There are lots of them, and many of them are hungry.

— Andy Grove, Intel Chairman and former CEO

The offshoring of technical support[1] has become a hot topic in the popular and business press. Shifting jobs from the domestic workforce to overseas providers is an emotionally charged topic for many people in the support world and beyond. But allowing the debate to become emotional, in my opinion, is a mistake. It prevents you from objectively viewing and assessing the value of all sides of the discussion. This debate is certainly worth having. Let's make sure you understand all sides.

Let's start by defining[2] the terms "offshoring" and "globalization."

Offshoring: The shifting of technical support delivery around the world. Note that this is a variation of outsourcing.

Globalization: The dissemination or distribution of business functions, irrespective of location, to optimize:

- The service experience of the customer or employee
- The cost of the delivery of that service, and
- The effectiveness & timeliness of service delivery

Why Offshoring?

Three factors are motivating the current offshoring phenomenon: pressures from global labor market, technology drivers and economic drivers.

Global Labor Market

As Intel's Andy Grove points out, there is a lot of competition for jobs around the world. In particular, vast pools of college-educated workers overseas are able and willing to work in customer support and service jobs. Employers in developed countries, by contrast, have a very hard time filling these jobs with qualified candidates.

When you think of employees in less-developed countries working for lower wages, some people conjure up images of a sweatshop. They imagine desperate people earning less than living wages, forced to work against their will in dank workplaces.

For support jobs at least, this is pretty far from the truth. For people in many developing nations, support jobs pay relatively well and offer tremendous benefits. Go to Bangalore, India, and visit one of the elaborate corporate campuses of IT companies. None of them would look out of place in Silicon Valley during the boom years. There are free cafeterias serving great food, vast training facilities that can instruct as many as 600 students per day, swimming pools, gyms, day care, laundry facilities and more. To compensate for Bangalore's less reliable infrastructure, most companies have their own backup electric generators and even water supplies.

However, with the explosion in jobs and escalating wages, even India is facing challenges. The turnover rate for Bangalore call center agents with undergraduate and Master's degrees is approaching 60%. Every senior HR executive I spoke to blames the job-hopping on the lure of more money from a competitor.

One senior HR executive at a top Indian company told me he wanted the signs outside changed from "Trespassers will be prosecuted" to "Trespassers will be recruited!" He was joking, of course – but only partially.

It is only a matter of time before India's current advantage in relatively inexpensive, highly skilled labor will be edged out by other up-and-coming-regions. Indian companies have already started preparing for that eventuality by forging strategic alliances in Eastern Europe, China and Africa. Many have been acquiring companies in Europe and the Far East, to enable them to tap into the special language requirements that currently cannot be easily sourced in India.

Another sleeping giant is China. After developing its manufacturing prowess, China is now looking enviously at India's huge lead in service excellence. Chinese companies are working hard to get their employees' language and technical skills up to speed. Learning English at Grade 3 is now mandatory in Chinese elementary schools.

Technology Drivers

Faster, better, cheaper technology is also fueling the offshoring boom. Every year, the "bang for the buck" factor – the amount of technology you can buy at a given price – soars. In addition, technology has become relatively easier to use.

One classic example is the Internet. In the early 1990s, very few Americans outside educational and research institutions had access to email or workplace collaboration tools, and using them practically required an advanced degree. Fast-forward just ten years to 2005. Millions of people have virtually forsaken "snail" mail and even phone calls for near-instantaneous communication with people around the world via email and instant messaging.

Another technological *tour de force* that is driving the offshoring phenomenon is VoIP. By slashing the cost of communication, Voice over IP allows companies and individuals to make long distance telephone calls via the Internet, for a fraction of the cost of land lines or even cell phones. Technology and communications are not the insurmountable barriers they seemed to be just ten years ago. All these technologies have driven down costs and enabled the offshoring of technical support.

Economic Drivers

Facing intense competition and a relentless pressure to control costs, executives in corporations everywhere are being asked to take a good look at their operations and cut any unnecessary expenditures. Labor is typically the largest expense in customer support, so it's not surprising that companies are taking steps to trim the fat. Some have chosen to drive down costs by automating support as much as possible. Other companies have chosen to offshore portions of their support. A few have embraced a combination of the two.

Since 2003, some venture capitalists have insisted that development and support plans include an offshore component before they'll fund new technology companies in the United States.

Issues to Consider Before Offshoring

Back Office

When senior executives consider outsourcing support, they often neglect to consider how their "back-office" systems will be synchronized with the offshore provider. Back-office systems, as you know, provide behind-the-scenes operational support to ensure a customer's request has been received and properly serviced.

For example, what issue-tracking or CRM systems will be used? How will the two systems share data? How will your customer data be shared with the external company, if at all? A daily feed? Full access to the data? How will authentication and security be handled? How will the data be stored? Who will have access to it? How will knowledge be captured and shared across the two organizations?

Complexity

Integrating different back-office systems is complex and challenging, but that's only the beginning. You must also ensure that your organization and the outsourcing company work together to give seamless service to your customers. The biggest obstacle to this smooth integration is miscommunication.

If keeping your own support team up to date on different IT or engineering changes on a day-to-day basis is difficult, then imagine how much more disciplined you will have to be to ensure that a third party is also kept fully up-to-date on all ongoing and upcoming issues.

Problems also arise on a more mundane level. For example, if staff and executives travel, will their pagers and cell phones work in different countries? What happens when the escalation path involves an executive who is on a 12 hour flight to Australia and cannot be reached?

The *easiest* support contracts to write with an offshore provider include metrics the support manager is comfortable with – average speed of answer, first time resolution and more. But these metrics only measure how well the support operation is being run, not how well the customer is being taken care of.

Offshoring contracts should include incentives for high customer satisfaction scores (as measured by an independent third-party) and reduction in call volumes. Otherwise, you are rewarding them for increasing the number of calls they receive.

Compliance

In the United States, Section 404 of the Sarbanes-Oxley Act requires American companies to prove they have a system of internal controls. When key processes are outsourced, you must also ensure that the outsourced company is also compliant with Sarbanes-Oxley in the work that they do for you.

If you are part of the financial industry, just about every country you do business in has special regulations that you must follow and comply with.

If your company does business within the European Union or with EU customers, you must also comply with its strict security standards about access to customer records. The EU's Data Protection Directive, among other things, regulates the buying and selling of personal data about European citizens. It requires websites to inform users when they collect data about them, and allows users to refuse disclosure. This directive is much stronger than current US standards. In fact, it is generally regarded as one of the toughest in the world.

Connectivity

Many people in the US and Europe mistakenly assume that technology is "best in the West," and that the rest of the world isn't even close. This is simply not the case in at least two areas relevant to technical support and customer service: cell phones (called mobile phones in most of the world) and high-speed Internet connectivity to the home.

According to the International Telecommunications Union, the US ranks only 11th among countries with high speed[3] connections.

The US lags far behind global leaders such as Korea and Japan. There, broadband is much faster and cheaper, thanks to more focused national policy, less cumbersome regulation, and more densely populated regions.

> *For example:* Consumers in Korea can purchase a 20 Mbps Internet connection for a little more than $50 a month, according to *Business Week*. That's 10 to 40 times faster than a typical US connection, where a 3 Mbps connection costs about $45 per month.

Cultural

We discussed a few relevant cultural implications in Chapter 8, titled *Global Support*. Many of the same lessons apply in an outsourcing relationship. If you're not careful, misunderstandings across cultures can easily derail the hard work you put into making an outsourcing project successful.

Most outsourcing arrangements call for an account manager and a project leader at the other company. Make sure each is familiar with the norms and culture of both your company and your country – and that your team is familiar with theirs. Increase your familiarity with the subtle and hidden aspects of their culture, and you'll greatly reduce the number of potential stumbling blocks.

In some countries with a high Power-Distance Index, for example, you may think people are agreeing with you because they're saying "Yes." But they may simply be acknowledging that they've heard you – not agreeing to do what you've asked. Make sure you know which.

Customer

One of the key messages of this book is to look at everything from your customer's point of view. This is extremely important when it comes to outsourcing. What good does it do to save money by offshoring if too many of your customers become dissatisfied and abandon you? Pay careful attention to what kind of support you plan to outsource, and the method by which that support will be provided. Then make sure it is in your customer's best interests.

In general, phone support is the hardest to offshore well. Even with accent neutralization, it usually becomes obvious when a support call is being handled by someone in another country. By contrast, electronic communication is by far the easiest to offshore, in terms of potential backlash.

If your primary customers are consumers or end users and you offshore phone support, you are more likely to face potential backlash, particularly if the quality of service declines. This is partially due to the differences in accents, but also because of the visceral impact of people who feel that they are speaking with someone who has taken away their (or a friend's) job.

Employee

If you truly consider employees your most important asset, stop obscuring what you are doing or planning to do about outsourcing or offshoring.

Be honest with them. If you are considering offshoring to augment internal resources, let them know. If your plan is to replace staff that leave by attrition with offshored resources, let them know that.

Don't let your staff find out that you are considering offshoring only when strangers show up in their cubicle asking to be trained. (Don't laugh. It's happened more often than you think in both outsourcing and offshoring situations!)

Work with your employees to help them understand what is going on and why, and what they can expect going forward.

If you lose the trust of your employees, it will very quickly show in their behavior to your customers. Trust, once lost, is very hard to regain.

Financial

The financial terms of an outsourcing contract are another important consideration. Payments between companies in different countries are made in one country's currency. What happens when the value of that currency fluctuates? If you anticipate, say, an overall 40% savings by offshoring, half of this saving can very easily be wiped out completely by normal currency fluctuations. Your company's finance team should be able to structure the contract to minimize your currency risk.

Geopolitical

When India and Pakistan were on the brink of war early in the 21st century, the IT world held its collective breath. Travel, particularly non-essential business travel to the Indian subcontinent, was restricted. Had the standoff lasted longer, there could have been immense damage to India's reputation as the premier destination for offshoring.

Your company's risk management department (or legal team) will be able to help you assess country-specific risks.

Once you get serious about offshoring and narrow it down to one or two countries, start reading the online newspapers of those country to get a good idea of what is going on there.

Privacy

Many companies are nervous about the confidentiality of the data that is offshored. In addition, many companies do *not* want the fact they have offshored support made public.

Earlier we discussed the EU's Data Protection Directive. Among other things, the DPD restricts the flow of information about Europeans to companies based in countries which have, in the view of the EU, more lax privacy standards.

Some offshore companies are starting to deal with the privacy issue very aggressively. Some have instituted strict sign-in and sign-out policies for employees. Their staffs are allowed no means to store computer data: no floppy disks, CD burners – not even pens or paper! – in case a staff member is tempted to jot down customer-specific details. Employees and visitors alike are often searched when entering and leaving offshoring facilities. Aggressive measures like these allow overseas companies to overcome the understandable concerns involved with offshoring.

Intellectual Property

Ensure that all intellectual property rights issues are clearly spelled out in any offshoring agreement. For example, who owns the rights to new programs that are jointly developed? Which court has jurisdiction if you have to dispute an issue?

Understand that in some countries, court cases can take years to come to trial. Conversely, some foreign companies are wary of what they consider to be overly litigious behavior in the United States.

Security

When people think of security in terms of outsourcing, they normally think of technical security. But another risk, often overlooked, is physical security.

Will your teams be safe and comfortable working in remote offices? In some countries, you may need armed bodyguards to protect you or your team from robbery or kidnapping. The US State Department or its equivalent in other countries are valuable sources to learn about a country's overall state of security.

Having said that, a word of caution. Sometimes these reports seem so alarming, you will be too scared to go to any foreign country! Many of the suggestions involve common sense, and are true in any country.

How CEOs Should Prepare

CEOs also have a major role in terms of thinking of outsourcing. Remember, your offhand comments on "why aren't we outsourcing support" could cause major ripple effects on staff morale.

Evaluate the True Potential Savings

Most top executives look at offshoring simply as a way to save money. They see reports that manpower costs in India and the Philippines, as examples, are one-fifth or even one-tenth of those in the US. These reports have created wildly optimistic expectations for cost savings. But as you have seen, there are other issues to consider, and other costs to factor in.

Done properly, offshoring can be very good for your company and your customers. But, if your only motive is to save money, you are in for a rude shock. If implemented correctly, typical savings are more in the 20% range, which is still substantial.

> *Tip:* One of the most important things to remember is this: *You must get your processes under control first, before you try to outsource them.* If you don't, your offshoring adventure will become an expensive disaster, often with very public and customer-impacting repercussions.

Evaluate How Critical Support is to Your Organization

As the CEO, you must measure the business value that service and support contributes. For example, if you charge for support, how much top-line revenue does it bring in?

Among larger companies, services typically generate more than a third of total corporate revenues. The percentage is even higher for large vendors like SAP and Oracle, where revenue from services often exceeds two-thirds of total revenues and an even larger share of profits.

Create a Blueprint for the Entire Portfolio of Services Needed for Next Two Years

Support executives and front-line staff in particular often feel whiplashed by the frequent changes in direction from top management. What they need, particularly in an area that could have a dramatic impact on their teams, is honesty and a long-term perspective.

You may think that you need to bring only a few people into the fold of potentially explosive discussions like offshoring. In reality, you should share information with your company's customer support leaders as soon as you can.

People, especially those whose career anchors cause them to value security over adventure, appreciate having a compass and map that tells them where they are going and provide a plan for how to get there. They will feel even more connected to your company's goals, and more invested in its future, when they can contribute to that plan and help you deliver on it.

How Support Executives Should Prepare

This advice is for executives that run support operations.

Functionality Core to a Business' Success is Likely to Stay In-House

Is your support operation a competitive differentiator? Does it add value? Do customers choose your company at least partially because of the quality of its customer service? The first thing you must work through with your organization's executive leadership is to answer those questions. Marketing consultant Geoffrey Moore[4] talks about it in terms of core and context. Core, says Moore, is whatever differentiates you and gives you a competitive edge. Everything else is context.

One of the most common mistakes support managers make is confusing *important* work from *core* work. Just because what you do is important, does not mean it is core work.

> *For example:* Think about payroll and how important that function is to running a business, and how sensitive that information is. It is vitally important – but is *not* core to most US businesses. Thus, payroll is routinely outsourced.

Develop Metrics on Quality & Quantity of Work for the Support of Business

Frankly, most support metrics are useless to the rest of your company, and certainly to its top executives. Yes, they are helpful for those managing a department, but they're usually not meaningful for anyone else. Most don't indicate how much customer support impacts your business, how much revenue it generates, or how much profit it brings in.

Instead, support performance is reported in terms like average speed of answer and call handling times. So what? These metrics don't really matter to customers or even co-workers beyond the service desk. After all, customers just want to make sure that their issues are resolved quickly. From their perspective, everything else is irrelevant.

> *Here is an eye-opening exercise* that might help you see how support is viewed by the rest of your company. For your next report, take the metrics that you regularly report on, and make a few changes to the three you think are most important to the rest of the company. Double the first two and divide the third one in half. Then sit back and see if anyone notices. If no one does, then your reporting metrics are irrelevant. Either you're reporting the wrong things, or you're presenting them in a way that the rest of the organization does not care about.

In reality, customer support professionals touch every other department more than anyone else in the company (with the possible exception of human resources). The problem is, customer support focuses completely on its own little world. You don't speak the same language as other departments or top management. They don't understand why it's important. Make it your job to tell them. Start by learning how to speak the language of the other departments, and speaking the language of the business which is ultimately about profitability.

When you're working with product engineering, for example, talk in their terms. And get specific. "The last three products had these five defects. We can't afford to have those problems again, and here are the reasons why. Removing those problems will reduce the number of calls coming in from this specific customer. It will save the customer this much money, and our company will save that much money."

No one really likes to correct defects, issue bug fixes or maintain existing products. It's much more fun and interesting to work on the new stuff. Explaining support issues in their terms helps the company and the engineers do that.

The same principle applies to every other department. Show them how a support issue affects their department, the customers, and the company's bottom line, and you'll quickly get their attention.

Show Significant and Ongoing Improvement in Productivity

As an Ultimate Customer Support Executive, you should be at the epicenter of just about everything customer-related that goes on in your company.

Most departments optimize their service around their own function. Unfortunately, these department-centric optimizations can lead to suboptimal customer experiences – and those are the most important ones! The way to fix this problem is to flip it around. View every process and situation from the customer's perspective first. Become the voice of the customer as you look at any customer-facing processes or products.

I recently spoke with a senior support executive at a major organization who was very proud of his team's high customer-satisfaction scores. When shown that those scores were completely out of synch with what his customers were saying on the Internet, he said, "Those are issues with other departments." Sorry, wrong answer. The customer is everyone's department. As an Ultimate Customer Support Executive, you are the face of the company to the largest number of customers. It's your responsibility to get problems resolved!

Involve Customers in All Changes to Your Support

If you keep your internal or external customers involved in what you are doing, they are more likely to view you as a partner. For example, if your technology company has built software tools that your customers can use to integrate your services into their operations, your customers may have either bought additional tools or written scripts or programs that plug into your tools.

So if you make changes to the tool, you may inadvertently break the scripts that they have written.

The solution: Be sure to publicize any changes well in advance, and give your customers and partners plenty of time before modifying or shutting down support for a product or service. I've seen multi-million dollar accounts jeopardized over something as simple as this, particularly when resellers are involved.

Develop a Strategic View to Align Corporate Priorities with the Needs of Your Employees

Balancing the needs of your company and your staff is tricky. As mentioned in Chapter 1, titled *Leadership*, too often junior support managers end up taking care of their employees at the expense of the corporation. This is a fatal flaw. If you look after a few, the many may be hurt.

Help your employees understand the big picture – what's going on in the company as a whole, not just their corner of it. Bring "guest stars" from other departments to your meetings to explain different concepts your team may not be familiar with, and how their support functions impact those concepts.

For example: Bring in the marketing manager to explain the goals for the corporate brand, and start a dialogue on how customer support can help with this.

Learn to Work with Distributed Teams

Distributed teams, in which team members work in different locations, are fast becoming commonplace in today's globally connected environment. Distributed teams face their own set of challenges and communication issues.

Learn how to manage remote teams, whether they are part of your organization, or an outsourced or offshored relationship. Many technical training facilities and consultants now offer classes on this topic.

How Front-Line Support Staff Should Prepare

If your front line staff are unhappy or unsure of your direction with outsourcing their jobs, this uncertainty and fear will almost certainly pass on to your customers.

Participate in Productivity Improvement Programs

The front lines can be a lonely place. Customer support is one of the few professions in the world where you are expected to listen to complaints and take abuse all day (and often all night). To top it off, your bosses don't seem to want you to stay. They encourage the best among you to learn about the business, then move on to other departments or divisions.

Then you hear about concepts like "self-service" and "great service," both designed to reduce the number of contacts customers have with you. *What*, you wonder? They don't want you to stay, and they want to take away your job – if not to automation, then to offshoring? Don't they want people to provide customer support anymore?

It can seem that customer support is going the way of automation, but look at it from a different perspective. Automation allows routine, repetitive calls and issues to be deflected before they reach you. That reduces the brain-numbing number of times you have to repeat the same thing, over and over, to customer after customer. The queries that remain will be more complex, more challenging ones.

Remember, too, what's going on in the company as a whole. Your managers and top executives are under mounting pressures, trying to compete in a global world. You can help them by not having a knee-jerk reaction to the concept of offshoring.

As a support person, you have a great advantage. Because you interact with customers, resellers and corporate partners, you learn about many issues facing your company. These insights give you a great opportunity to add value and even boost revenues. Use your ideas, imagination and creativity. Help your management see, for example, how investing $1 in support could save $15 elsewhere in the company. That's adding value to the organization!

Study Important Issues and Participate in Dialogues

If your job may potentially be outsourced or impacted by changes, people will assume that you are going to react a certain way – typically, by being defensive. You can defuse or completely negate this by being very open-minded to both sides of the dialogue. If everything you say is perceived to be negative, people will eventually exclude you from the dialogue. That's not what you want.

Keep up with different initiatives going on inside the company. Start by taking another look at Chapter 6, titled *Process,* for different processes and initiatives that might already be underway within your organization.

Prepare for New Roles by Learning New Skills

New roles often open up for a good support person. In addition to your technical prowess, you are probably also adept at certain so-called "soft" skills. These are "people skills," like listening to a customer, multi-tasking, remaining calm under pressure and having a positive, can-do attitude. These skills are timeless and invaluable. Best of all, they can easily be transferred to other departments or positions. Keep perfecting those skills; they will stand you in good stead – in support or beyond.

Get certified in support and technology skills. Get certified as a Help Desk Analyst from one of the organizations offering certification. Many employers provide tuition reimbursement and/or time off to take classes like these. Take advantage of these opportunities. Upgrade your skills and you increase your value.

There are plenty of departments outside support that need talented people who understand the customer's needs and can apply the principles of support throughout the organization. These include areas like business continuity, release and change management, etc.

Your skills and knowledge can also be valuable in a training capacity. Offer to reach out and train others, including partners and resellers.

Final Thoughts

Offshoring isn't right for every organization. But if planned and implemented properly, offshoring can save many companies 20–40%, after you factor in the costs of things like systems infrastructure development, back-office integration, and privacy.

The key to success is planning. Think it through carefully. Only outsource those things that your teams do not add value to, and which make sense in the context of your customers. If you do that, it can work quite well.

The root cause of most failed outsourcing or offshoring attempts is the company's existing internal support processes. In all likelihood, they were poorly designed to begin with. If so, any outsourcing initiatives were doomed to fail.

The fear and furor over offshoring will die down, I predict, much like the Japan/Detroit "car wars" of the 1980s. Back then, Americans were concerned that Japanese cars were gaining market share very quickly. There were angry calls to "Buy American."

Today, this is practically a non-issue. Auto parts are manufactured all over the world and assembled in multiple locations. Different car companies own each other. Chrysler was bought by Daimler, makers of Mercedes Benz. It's hard to even tell what a "foreign" car is anymore. Toyotas are made in

California, while Chrysler mini-vans are assembled in Canada. All most people want now is a quality vehicle, at the right price.

It's the same in customer support. All customers really want is a solid, dependable service experience that answers their questions quickly and correctly, and lets them get back to work.

10 Being Recognized

My grandfather once told me that there were two kinds of people: those who do the work and those who take the credit. He told me to try to be in the first group; there was much less competition.

– Indira Gandhi, former Prime Minister of India

If you've read this far, you've learned that your role as the Ultimate Customer Support Executive is to be your customer's champion, your company's champion and your staff's champion. You know that you must demonstrate leadership that goes beyond operational excellence and incorporates passion for what you do.

You must know how to get the most out of people, smash customer-unfriendly processes, use technology judiciously and make your entire organization customer-friendly.

You are *almost* there! As a support executive, you probably spend a lot of time trying to get a "seat at the table." But once you finally get the invitation, you may have trouble relating to the others at the table, or even know what to say.

There is one last, important step in your journey to becoming the Ultimate Customer Support Executive – *earning* respect, then *demanding* respect – from the rest of the company.

Earning Respect

On a professional level, to *earn* respect you must:

- Deliver results
- Know the business of the business
- Know how to work with key groups in the business
- Speak the language of the business
- Contribute to the company's bottom line, and ideally to the top line

Sometimes you have to earn respect by getting external validation of your efforts, such as support center site certification or customer support awards.

You can go on to *demand* respect when you are seen as the conscience of your company on behalf of the customer.

Deliver Results

In order to be an Ultimate Customer Support Executive, you have to deliver what is expected of you – every time, no excuses.

This means that at a minimum, your profitable customers are loyal and are champions for your service. If you provide internal support, that means that your most important customers (as measured by their impact on the business) are happy and productive, thanks to the work that you enable on their behalf.

Delivering results is important across multiple dimensions:

- The customer satisfaction dimension. They key question here is, *Are you doing the right things for your customer?* If the answer is yes, your profitable external customers and key internal customers are loyal, and act as evangelists for your service and company.
- The company dimension. They key question here is, *Are you doing the right things for your company?* If the answer is yes, you think of your company first, and give the

customer what they *need* rather than always giving them what they *want*. This means learning how to say no at the right times, and balancing quality of service with operational efficiencies.

- The team dimension. They key question here is, *Are you doing the right things for your team?* This means taking care of your team, standing up for them and developing your team.

Your metrics and reports should reflect consistent and solid scores across all these dimensions.

Know the Business of Your Business

To be an Ultimate Customer Support Executive, you must know the business of your business. You must understand what the company does, how it makes its money and where customer support fits into it. You need to see the big picture. Here is a good test to see if you really know the business of your business: Can you (or your senior team) clearly articulate why your customers purchase from you? What are your customers trying to accomplish by using your products or services? Who are your key competitors? What are the main differentiators for your company, the things that make you unique? If you cannot answer these questions, you do not really understand the business of your business.

To be an Ultimate Customer Support Executive, you must be an excellent ambassador for your organization. Here are some examples of what this means:

- The marketing department seeks you out to be the company spokesperson for speaking opportunities that are outside support. (In the case of a non-profit organization, you may be asked to represent the organization before potential donors.)

- When top prospects or customers visit your company, you are asked to be the lead executive sponsoring their visit, not just present the support dog-and-pony show.
- When potential business partners or resellers are deciding whether to partner with you and performing their due diligence, you are asked to be part of the key executive team that is involved.

Know How to Work with Key Groups

You've probably encountered people who are very knowledgeable in their field, but don't know much outside their area of expertise. Because of the sheer number of internal and external groups you touch, you have tremendous opportunities to shatter that stereotype and show others you are knowledgeable in more than one area.

Unfortunately, support personnel often only work with other groups in a reactive mode, i.e., when they want something.

In order to demonstrate your varied expertise and wield more influence, learn who the key groups are in your organization, and how to work with them. Below are important departments found in most organizations. Use this as a guideline to seek out key groups in your own organization.

Executive Management

This refers to the most senior set of executives in your organization. From a support perspective, their most important role is to articulate the importance of service and support to the rest of the company. But rhetoric isn't enough. Their commitment must also be demonstrated through their deeds – particularly funding key projects that turbocharge productivity.

As an Ultimate Customer Support Executive, your job is to make it easy for them to communicate the importance of service and support throughout the organization. Take the time to understand what is on each of their minds, and what their priorities and pet projects are. Are they detail-oriented, or "big picture"-oriented? Make sure that you tailor your communications to each one appropriately.

> *Tip:* Invite members of your executive management team to the front lines of customer support, to listen in on customer interactions.[1] Assure them that they will not be embarrassed in any way. Explain how important this is for your team's morale. This can also be effective company PR. What does it say about your company if your senior executives are in direct touch with their customers by periodically staffing the support lines?

There is another way you can significantly help senior management and at the same time benefit your team. Top managers sometimes try to be heroes, and jump in to resolve an apparent customer issue. In the process, unfortunately, they sometimes make promises that cannot be met. You must prevent them from doing that. Here's how.

Typically, this happens when the executive meets with a customer who surprises them with a litany of issues with your company. Just like everyone else, senior executives dislike being surprised with unpleasant information. Without specific, detailed information, they can only promise to resolve it, and apologize on behalf of the company. It is quite possible that the problem has nothing to do with your support team, or even your company. It is at these uncomfortable moments that top managers might overstep (and overpromise) what your team will do to resolve the issue.

The best way to avoid this is to prep senior executives before they meet with a customer. (If you do not know their schedule, talk with your counterpart in sales. They will certainly know if the boss is meeting with customers or prospects.) This will prevent senior management from being "ambushed" by customers bringing up issues. With your help and preparation, they will already know details of what is going on with that particular customer, and can clearly articulate the situation as well as what is being done to resolve any issues.

Sales

Sales people typically speak only one language – money. They are recruited and rewarded for their ability to close deals and bring in revenue, not for teamwork.

Top sales people are compensated very generously if they meet or exceed their sales quota. Those who consistently don't are simply let go. Salespeople are very transaction-oriented, which means that they are focused on the task at hand. So the way to communicate successfully with a sales rep is to help them achieve their immediate goal, and then get out of the way.

They are not interested in detailed updates on issues that they ask you about, unless their sale or upgrade is in jeopardy. However, once the pressure is off, the best salespeople always want additional information about their customer – information that you often have, since you deal with them throughout the customer lifecycle.

Customer support should be joined at the hip with sales leadership. Why? Revenue rules! It's that simple.

Tip: How do you find out more about what goes on inside the often rambunctious world of sales? Talk to your counterpart in sales. Ask if you can start attending sales forecast meetings, or at the very least, get the weekly or monthly sales forecast. Sales leadership is likely to agree if they see you as adding value to their discussions.

One way of adding value is to use your knowledge of existing customers to help them keep or upgrade a customer. Customers often tell different things to sales and support, particularly while negotiating renewals. Sharing this knowledge could help your sales rep choose a different, more effective approach while working with the customer.

Engineering

Engineering is a data-driven group. This is a team that will be glad to see metrics, particularly when they are presented in way that makes sense to them. They are comfortable with intuition only if it can be backed by numbers and logic.

Their debates are characterized by logic, not emotion. They can be passionate about their ideas, and ruthless in the way they tear apart what they consider an ill-constructed argument. That's OK. Remember, they are not attacking *you*, just your argument.

Stay calm. Getting emotional will not win any debates. Stick to the facts and stand your ground with well researched data. If your argument is sound, they will listen. Challenge and confront when appropriate. But do your homework. The better you know the underlying technology, the more respect you will earn.

Engineering is typically starved of direct customer input. The members of the team only get this information from groups like marketing and product development.

Help them understand what is going on by showing them exactly what customers are telling you about the code they've written or the product they have developed and how well it works. Invite them to visit customer support and take incoming queries from customers, to see firsthand how their work is being received in the marketplace. If they are reluctant to do this on a regular basis, talk to the head of the department about making it a requirement when new products or services are released. This will give them immediate feedback on their work, as well as insure you a place in future planning sessions.

Tip: You can help nudge things along by using engineers' competitive nature as a motivator. In your weekly reports, list top bugs by engineering group, and how long it takes each to get resolved. This will typically spark a fierce competition to get off this list as quickly as possible. But give equal time to the positive side, too. List features that customers and resellers like and why, and how using those features helps the customer's business.

Business Development

Business Development is the team that seeks out new revenue streams for your company. This may involve partnering with another company, acquiring or investing in a company or joint ventures, both domestic and international. Get to know your Business Development team. They can significantly impact your operation, but they inherently do not speak the language of support.

Reach out to them. Work with them in advance of their deals to help articulate what support does, and all the customer-impacting things that they will need prior to an impending merger, acquisition, new reseller partnership, etc.

> *Tip:* The best way to get their attention is to help them to evaluate a complex transaction thoroughly. Most high-tech mergers and acquisitions fail, often because of poorly thought-out customer service and support. They do not want a seemingly attractive deal to blow up in a little while, because it will reflect poorly on them.

Support executives can be a significant resource to them, because you touch so many parts of the company. You can help them think through issues that they may not have considered. For example, one of the typical reasons for an acquisition is to get the acquired company's customer base. You can help evaluate it closely to see if it is as valuable as the company claims it is. This input could substantially affect the value of the deal.

If you earn their trust, they are likely to include you in key steps in the business development process, like writing appropriate support clauses in the contracts. That will save you a lot of time and trouble trying to retroactively resolve issues that should have been addressed in the contract.

Finance

Finance as an organization is under intense pressure these days. Well publicized corporate accounting scandals have led to increased scrutiny and subsequent legislation, like Sarbanes Oxley in the US.

Support managers typically don't know much about finance, beyond the obvious fact that they keep a keen eye on a company's expenses. Naturally, the customer support team will be in their crosshairs; the tools you need are often capital intensive and require expensive consulting to implement. (It does not need to be this way, but that is usually the case with large implementations.)

> *Tip:* You can work better with Finance in at least one key area. In an era of doing more with less, many internal groups intensely lobby support to ensure that their "important" customer or prospect base is taken care of. The reality is that they may be important for a particular team, but not for the company as a whole.
>
> By partnering with Finance, an Ultimate Customer Support Executive can help them make the call about which competing resource is more deserving of scarce resources. Together, come up with a customer and prospect ranking system that clearly indicates to all company executives which customer or prospect is most important to the company.
>
> This can be as simple as a High/Medium/Low rating, based on the value of the customer or prospect. Incorporate this in a simple dashboard application that's accessible to your entire support team, and you will have a way to adjudicate these urgent requests for special favors that are above and beyond what your resources can handle. Rather than debate which request is more important, everyone can see the customer value rating and agree on the priority of the work to be done.

Legal

The Legal Department's primary duty is to reduce legal exposure for the company – i.e., to avoid risk.

The legal team can be a fantastic ally for support. Sales, under intense pressure to close the deal, will often change the terms of support contracts without your knowledge, in order to meet special requirements of a particular company. Inform Legal that you must sign off on any changes to the standard support contract template.

> *Tip:* Legal can also be a safety valve. They can pull you into a deal when other groups forget to include you, e.g., business development deals. Once Legal understands that you are trying to protect the company's reputation and the customer's well-being, they often become support's biggest internal champions.

Human Resources

As we've discussed before, customer support is a very people-dependent business. Human Resources is an often overlooked ally. Chances are, you think of HR (and perhaps not that fondly!) only when recruiting candidates or during annual performance reviews or salary increases. It does not need to be that way. They can be a very powerful ally.

If you're not pleased with the quality or quantity of candidates you're getting, it is your responsibility to work with HR to ensure that they understand exactly the kind of candidate you're looking for. Give them a candidate profile. Offer feedback on the candidates they deliver. It will help them hone in on exactly what you want. Finding the right candidate with the right temperament and skills is hard enough. Don't make a difficult situation worse by not enabling HR to succeed.

Often you will find that your support team is on the cutting edge of what HR allows. For example, support may be one of the first groups in the company that allows people to work from home. It might make sense to ensure coverage during inclement weather, for example. Understand, however, that HR will worry about setting a dangerous precedent. Talk to them early and give them time to make the changes needed.

> *Tip:* HR can also boost your training budget. For example, they may be able to leverage your need for customer service training across other groups by

bringing in a trainer that can benefit several departments. If the training offers company-wide benefits, it will often come out of their budget instead of yours. This frees up more of your limited training budget for specific customer support requirements. You can and should extend this type of training partnership to other groups in your company.

Resellers

As mentioned earlier, resellers are important because they extend your company's sales reach, often without anyone in support involved in how the reseller provides support. Yet when new products or services are launched, resellers often have to remind the company to think of them.

You can help the reseller team by reminding the rest of the company that all products and services should be designed, right from the start, to be "reseller ready." From a customer support point of view, this means that the reseller's support team should be self-sufficient from the day the product or service is launched. If the reseller has tools and visibility into the products or services, they need to be developed and ready at launch. As a bonus, this approach automatically ensures that your own customer support team has everything they need in order to support the product or service.

> *Tip:* You can potentially save your company a lot of money by inspecting the customer support lifecycle for the reseller and distributor channels. Most companies treat reseller revenue as profitable revenue. This may be true, if support costs are under control. Unfortunately, this is often not the case.

Most support and distribution arrangements are made with little in-depth understanding of the costs of maintaining the resold customer or distributor. Costs for training, documentation, planning and escalation are often not considered. In addition, there is frequently no control over the quality of support provided by the reseller or the distributor. Their inadequate support could do tremendous damage to your organization's reputation, so it should be carefully considered.

One way around this problem is to ensure that the support expectations are clearly spelled out during contract negotiations or when they come up for renegotiation.

Speak the Language of the Business

The most common barrier that prevents a support executive from becoming the Ultimate Customer Support Executive is not being able to speak the language of business. Each department may have its own terminology and acronyms, but the fundamental language of any business is money.

Understanding Financial Statements

One of the best ways to learn to speak the language of money is to understand financial statements. Below are some basic terms for those of you who are not familiar with budgeting beyond justifying your headcount.

Balance Sheet: Assets = Liability + Equity

Looking at a company's balance sheet gives you a good overview of the company's financial health. A balance sheet reveals what assets it holds, both real (such as factories or land) and intangible (such as goodwill). It also shows how these assets are funded, either through shareholder equity or debt.

Shareholder equity is the value of the owner's stake in the company at historic values. This usually bears little resemblance to what the shareholders will get if the company is sold – that's the market value.

A balance sheet is also useful for discovering a company's net assets. These are its current assets (what it owns, i.e., short term assets such as cash, receivables, prepayments) less its current liabilities (what it owes, i.e., payables, accruals). The net figure is sometimes referred to as working capital. You want to see a positive balance here.

Income Statement

Read an income statement from top to bottom. The first line (or top line) lists all the revenue brought in, while each subsequent line deducts various expenses and cost. The last line (or bottom line) refers to net income. Aha! Now you know where the terms "top line" and "bottom line" come from.

A sample income statement includes the following terms:

- Revenue: Sales
- Cost of Goods Sold (COGS): As the name implies, COGS is essentially the cost of producing or acquiring something you sell.
- Gross Margin (GM): Revenue minus COGS
- Operating Expenses (OE): All expenses that don't neatly fall under COGS
- Net Income Before Interest and Taxes: Gross Margin minus Operating Expenses
- Interest Expense: Payments on loans and other debt
- Income Tax Expense: Amount of tax to be paid to federal and state governments
- Net Income: Profit after all other expenses are taken out
- Net Income Per Share: Net Income divided by the number of shares

Cash Flow Statement

Another important statement, the cash flow statement strips out anything not cash related (such as depreciation) from the income statement. It is usually shown in three parts: cash from operating, financing and investing. The ability to generate cash is commonly seen as the most important indicator of a company's financial health.

Financial Ratios

There are many financial ratios used to evaluate companies and their financial health.

- Days Sales Outstanding (DSO): This is a measure of how quickly a customer is paying you. The premise is that happy customers consider your products essential and are more likely to pay than unhappy ones.
- Profit Margin: The ratio of net income to revenues
- Income per Employee: A measure of productivity
- Return on Capital: Net Income divided by Shareholders Equity
- Return on Assets: Net income divided by total fixed assets. This is particularly useful for asset-intensive businesses.

Contribute to the Bottom Line, and Ideally to the Top Line

One of the best ways to earn respect from higher-ups is to move beyond just cutting costs. Start bringing in revenue.

In an external support environment, customer support profit margins can be very high – comparable to license margins in software companies with very large installed bases. After all, it is typically far more profitable to sell a 1,000 user license of some software to a customer than it is a 100 user license of the same software to the same customer as it doesn't really cost your company that much more. Better yet, since support revenue comes largely from renewals, it's both more stable and more predictable than license revenue.

Among larger software companies, services, including service and support, typically generate more than a third of total corporate revenues. The percentage is even higher for large vendors like SAP and Oracle. There it exceeds two-thirds of revenues and a substantially larger share of profits.

In general, according to the SSPA, support and maintenance contracts contribute as much as 60% of a vendor's profitability. A pretty rosy picture from the vendor's perspective. Unfortunately, the view is not the same from the customer side of the fence.

Many CIOs, for example, hate paying maintenance fees. Typically, customers pay a percentage of the list price of a software license every year for support and maintenance. This backlash puts pressure on you to better articulate the value that support delivers to customers, so they don't just see it as a necessary evil.

Another technique to improving your top line growth is to work with your Professional Services team to see if your support staff can take on some of the work that they do, enabling them to concentrate on bringing in higher-margin revenue.

A more traditional way to contribute to your company's bottom line is by achieving additional savings. While cost-cutting continues to be important, I'd urge you to shift *where* you focus the majority of your efforts. As a customer support executive, you are no doubt skilled at attacking the *symptoms* of problems so they are resolved faster, and making sure the customer is happy while you do it. Use these same skills to boost your service to a higher level. Spend the majority of your time looking for ways to reduce or even eliminate customer-impacting issues before they impact the customer. Preventing problems will save far more time and money – and improve customer satisfaction – than merely fixing them. As we discussed earlier, this is the difference between providing *good* service (taking care of someone after they contact you with an issue) and *great* service (ensuring they don't have issues in the first place).

External Validation

Sometimes, despite all that you do, you will not get the respect you deserve until an independent organization recognizes and certifies your achievements. There's nothing like an external group proclaiming that you are among the best in the world at what you do to wake up your own organization, existing customers and potential clients.

There are two ways to get this external validation.[2] One is to get your entire Support Center "site certified." The other is for your customer support center to win a few specific awards.

Support Center Site Certification

Two different groups give technology support site certifications, based on their assessments of your operations.[3] These are:

- *Support Center Certification (SCC) from HDI.*[4] The SCC program consists of 8 core areas that contain 66 statements. The core areas include enabling factors (leadership, policy and strategy, people management, resources, and process and procedure) and results (people satisfaction, customer satisfaction and performance results).

  Four levels of maturity exist for each of the standard statements, and weighted scoring determines the overall effectiveness and success of the support organization. HDI's SCC requires an on-site audit to ensure that companies meet the scores required for certification. In order to maintain certification status, companies must continue their commitment to the HDI SCC program and its standards through annual mini-audits.

- *Support Center Practices (SCP) from Service Strategies.*[5] Support Strategies offers two certifications, one for Customer Support, and another for Professional Services and Field Services.

A technology support organization must meet minimum performance standards for customer satisfaction in order to achieve SCP Certification. SCP Certification then requires comprehensive on-site audits to confirm that you have met the requirements of the over 100 business elements defined in the program. SCP Certified companies must then continue to demonstrate their ongoing commitment to excellence and high performance standards through annual re-certification audits.

Customer Support Awards

Several organizations, both in the US and overseas, host customer service competitions that your organization can enter. Winning an award is gratifying, and the external validation can help you earn more respect from your staff, colleagues and superiors.

- The Association of Support Professionals[6] has a highly regarded *Best Web Support Sites* competition. Entering this competition will help you see what others in the support profession see as a best-of-breed web support site.
- HDI holds the *Team Excellence Awards* for both internal and external support teams.
- The SSPA[7] has the *STAR Awards* in a number of different categories, including complex support, high call volume and more.

In addition, many international support associations are starting to offer awards of their own. Check them out!

Demanding Respect

A "No" uttered from deepest conviction is better and greater than a "Yes" merely uttered to please, or what is worse, to avoid trouble.

– Mahatma Gandhi

After you have *earned* respect, it is time to *demand* respect. As the ultimate customer champion, you owe it to the customer to demand respect. In order to demand respect (after you have earned it), you must be seen as the conscience of your company on behalf of the customer.

Being the Conscience of Your Company on Behalf of the Customer

You'll know you've reached this stage when people in your company stop and think about what you would say on behalf of the customer before they do something – even when you're not there.

To get to this level, being respected is not enough. You have to make sure that a few of your strengths – your likeability and desire to make others happy – are not seen as weaknesses.

This means that you have to start standing up for your customers, your teams and yourself. Admittedly, this is not something that comes naturally to most support leaders. You probably prefer to avoid confrontation. Get over it! Challenge other groups and leaders. Challenge them with respect, certainly, but challenge if you must, on behalf of your customers.

For example, don't allow IT, Engineering or Product Development to release products or services without your knowledge. Don't let them hide developments from you until they are very close to launch date, well after all decisions have been made. When you identify a root cause for a problem, be relentless in your pursuit of it being resolved, particularly once it has been prioritized as a top customer-impacting issue. Do not accept vague promises about the priority or resources assigned to resolving them.

Sometimes this involves a change in perspective. Let's say, for example, you want to open up some of your internal customer support troubleshooting tools for customers and reseller partners to use, but your security team balks. Assuming that this is important to the company, don't simply accept this pushback from Security and back off. Instead, put the impetus for resolving the issue on Security. Clearly articulate what you want done, and ask for a timeline when all security issues will be resolved so that customers and reseller partners can get access to your troubleshooting tools. Demand respect!

Interviews

Jennifer Ash

Jennifer Ash is an organizational consulting psychologist whose company, Psipher Consulting, helps decode the secrets of executive success.

Q: As both an HR expert and a psychologist, Jennifer, can you offer some suggestions for customer support executives? In what areas do they need to improve?

A: Research has shown that the traits that make a good customer support executive – likeability, empathy and the ability to build relationships – can end up getting in your way when it comes to leading and managing others.

These traits are admirable and for the individual contributor, no doubt lead to good customer service. However, for leadership roles, these personal characteristics can get in the way of doing good business. For one thing, customer support executives often are seen as not consistently holding people accountable.

Another area is that customer support executives often don't know when to push back. If this is not addressed, you may become known as a person who will back down, rather than deal with an uncomfortable situation. It's because of your innate desire to please. Know how you are being perceived, because perception becomes reality.

Jeff Tarter

Jeff Tarter is founder of the Association of Support Professionals, and a respected industry expert.

Q: What have been some of the characteristics of some of the most successful support executives you know?

A: Their ability to look at everything from a customer's perspective. They are marketing focused, inherently entrepreneurial in nature (particularly if they run external support groups), operations focused, know how to run their business, a little bit of a cowboy in terms of risk taking, and are polished executives that could run just about any group in the company.

Ron Muns

Ron Muns is the CEO and Founder of Help Desk Institute.

Q: What have been some of the characteristics of some of the most successful support executives you know?

A: They have a balanced approach to job responsibilities. They focus on business, have a mastery of operations and manage to stay strategic. They are good coaches, leaders and mentors to the people doing the work.

They are energetic, enthusiastic. They love what they do, and it shows. They are not afraid to innovate, change, break things up.

Malcolm Fry

Malcolm Fry is a respected support industry expert and consultant based in the UK.

Q: What have been some of the characteristics of some of the most successful support executives you know?

A: Attitude. There is no such thing as a "good" call to customer support. But you still have to be positive.
Communication – and not just when things are going badly. Their ability to make metrics very simple for everyone to understand and communicate.

Bill Rose

Bill is the founder and Executive Chairman of the Service & Support Professionals Association.

Q: What have been some of the characteristics of some of the most successful support executives you know?

A: First, they must be able to understand technology and be excellent trouble shooters. As managers, they have to know their numbers really well, and be able to manage up. They must be able to lobby effectively to get the resources their department needs. Most need to become more business oriented. A good support executive has good people skills, too. They have to be able to motivate and cultivate the people in their organization.

Ed Hawthorne

Ed Hawthorne is a Senior Vice President and Emerging Operational Risk Executive at the Bank of America.

Q: Ed, you more or less epitomize the concept of the Ultimate Customer Support Executive. You started out as a programmer, then moved into support, and are now a senior executive at a Fortune 100 company. How should someone decide on new career opportunities?"

A: In general, I use the following criteria to evaluate new opportunities.

- *Challenge* – Does the job challenge me enough professionally to keep me motivated?
- *Growth* – Does the job offer me enough growth and development?
- *Impact* – What kind of impact can I make to the company, my associates, and your shareholders and customers?

Q: Ed, what suggestions do you have for a mid level support executive who wants to get to the next level?

A: Make sure that you have a deep understanding of your business, and consistently demonstrate leadership. Don't be afraid to take prudent risks. Be prepared.

As support executives, you have an innate ability to connect things and people. Use this for the betterment of your customers, your associates and your organization.

Seek out and find mentors, experienced people in different areas in your organization (and outside!) who can help you with your career and help you see things in a different way. Be a mentor to others, too. You will not only teach, you will learn in this process as well.

I would wrap it all with the big "I" – Integrity. Operate with integrity. Never do anything that compromises it. Your customers and associates will see right through it. Never, ever do it!

11 *Future*

*In a few hundred years, when the history of our time will be
written from a long-term perspective, it is likely that the most
important event historians will see is not technology, not the
Internet, not e-commerce. It is an unprecedented change in the
human condition. For the first time — literally — substantial
and rapidly growing numbers of people have choices. For the
first time, they will have to manage themselves. And society
is totally unprepared for it.*

– Peter F. Drucker, management guru

Who has the time to think about the future? In customer
support, most of our time is consumed with taking care
of customer issues (which are inherently time-sensitive and
disruptive) and attending meetings. When do we get the luxury
of thinking 10 years out? How can we start preparing for the
future when we barely have enough time to deal with everything
the present has thrown at us?

The question itself is precisely the reason why we should
start thinking about and preparing for the future *now*. If we
don't envision a future and start creating it, someone else will
do it for us. If history is any guide, abdicating this opportunity
means the future will not be a pleasant one — for you or the
customers you represent. If we are truly to become Ultimate
Customer Support Executives, we must make the time to look
intelligently at what the future holds.

While the three pillars of customer support are traditionally people, process and technology, I'd like to begin with technology predictions, then follow with people and process predictions. That approach will better explain the profound changes that are coming, especially on the people and process sides of the support equation. I'll also introduce you to a very powerful technique called "scenario planning," which we used while I was chairperson of HDI's Strategic Advisory Board to help us predict possible scenarios for customer support in 2015.

Technology Predictions

The trend towards smaller, faster, cheaper and always connected technology is already well documented. But let's spend a moment looking at its future impact on customer support.

Technology Will Change the Lives of Millions

As time goes by, many inexpensive new technologies will reach out and embrace millions more in the future. A few of these technologies include WiMax,[1] which can provide wireless Internet coverage over a radius of 30 miles, compared to the 300-foot range of the now-common 802.11b standard. WiMax will help push adoption of high speed internet in the developed world.

Another standard, ZigBee,[2] allows a variety of low-power devices to communicate over an unregulated portion of the radio spectrum. Other technologies in this category include cell-phones, Bluetooth[3] and Wi-Fi.[4] But unlike those three (and others that use the unregulated portion of the radio spectrum), ZigBee devices can run for years on inexpensive batteries, eliminating the need to be plugged into electrical power. ZigBee shows great promise in areas like energy conservation (*Is anyone in the house? Do I need to leave the air conditioning on?*) and agriculture (*Does the crop need water?*)

RFID, which stands for Radio Frequency Identification, will also extend the state of "the internet of things" and "always on." Utilizing a microchip the size of a grain of sand, RFID chips contain data that can be transmitted automatically over radio waves, making it possible to track items without costly manual scanning. RFID tags are affixed to all kinds of items, from mammoth shipping containers to individual consumer goods on store shelves. Networks of RFID tag readers – on shipping docks, inside trucks, and on grocery store shelves – instantly communicate the whereabouts of any individual product. Proponents believe that RFID will soon replace printed bar codes on most products. Retailers expect to save billions, reduce theft and improve inventory management.

RFID is the one of the most innovative technologies of the past 25 years, according to researchers at MIT's Lemelsen Center. CNN's *The Top 25 Innovations of the Last 25 Years* saluted the internet, cell phones, personal computers, fiber optics, email and digital cameras as among the technologies that have most changed our lives.

When we think about the future, most of us visualize a technologically rich society, increasingly interconnected and interdependent. While this is certainly true for most readers of this book, don't forget that more than 4 billion people in the world have a purchasing power of less than $4 a day. These people face unpredictable power supplies, dusty work environments, erratic communications networks, language barriers and many more challenges. As cheaper technology reaches this large and very diverse segment of society, profound societal changes will occur. To serve them, we will have to come up with many innovations in the people, process and technology aspects of customer support.

The cost of many products and services will need to drop so low that if they don't work, they'll simply be thrown away. Most of us mistakenly assume that cheaper technology means inferior technology, and that innovation always trickles down. In reality, this doesn't need to be the case. As the adage goes, "Necessity is the mother of invention."

Example of Innovation Moving Up

Consider the challenges required to make technology accessible to the millions of people who don't speak the language of their countries' elite. Millions would be rendered functionally illiterate simply because they can't read the language used by a computer.

Now consider Prodem, a company which markets bank Automatic Teller Machines in Bolivia. Prodem ATMs recognize that many Bolivians speak one of three languages: Spanish, or one of the two predominant indigenous languages, Aymara and Quechua. In addition to accommodating all three languages, Prodem ATMs sport a rich visual interface[5] that makes them easy to use even if you don't speak any of them. They utilize both smart card technology as well as fingerprint access to each customer's account. A major advantage of smart cards is that the customer's personal details, account numbers, record of transactions and fingerprint are stored right on the card, not on a far-off central server. This allows the cash dispensers to operate even without a permanent network connection, which is often a luxury in remote areas of the world. Prodem's ATM machines also cost less than one-third of the price of a typical ATM machine in the United States.

This is a good example of using biometric passwords and intuitive user interfaces even at very low price points. Solutions like these, I believe, will not only serve developing nations, but also push progress *up* the economic chain. Soon we, too, may enjoy access to biometric technology, such as fingerprints, retina scans and voice recognition. One day we'll no longer have to remember dozens or even hundreds of passwords.

> *Example:* Social changes are already happening. Consider India. It literally used to take years – and often a well-placed bribe – to get a traditional (landline) phone installed in a home. Today India boasts about one million new cellular phone users every month, and growing. In many remote villages, the phenomenal growth of mobile phones has even changed the centuries-old power structures. Now, for example, a

disenfranchised rural woman might get a mobile phone, then resell some of her phone time to fellow villagers for a low per-minute fee that is affordable, yet still high enough to enable her to make a healthy living. This changes not just her economic status, but also her social status. She now plays a vital role in her village, whereas before she may have been marginalized.

People Predictions

If we are successful in our quest to unleash the power of the customer within the organization, we will see a rise in popularity of a relatively new position: the Chief Customer Officer (CCO).

Chief Customer Officer

Reporting directly to the CEO, this executive ensures that the power of the customer resonates throughout an organization.

The CCO's responsibilities encompass the entire customer lifecycle. A major component of the job is to attract profitable customers and keep them for life. It differs from current customer support roles, which for the most part are inherently post-sales. While many people in an organization care about the customer, their point of view is typically from the context of their own departmental boundaries. In contrast, the CCO will have the organizational clout and experience to reach across organizational silos and ensure that things are always considered from the customer's perspective.

In the future, I see both internal and external support teams reporting to this one executive. Today, each support team almost always reports to a different group. Internal customer support most often reports to the CIO, while the external support group usually reports to sales or engineering, and sometimes directly to the Chief Operating Officer.

Process Predictions

Both internal and external support build off the same fundamental principles: people, process and technology. The biggest differences today exist within processes. Internal support processes are usually more developed than those of external support. This makes sense. In general, it is easier to get your own company or organization to adopt standards and rules than convincing an external customer to do so. Having worked in and managed both kinds of teams, I can say with certainty that each can learn a lot from the other.

In the future, I predict only two classes of support will be needed in the world of technology. All remaining types of support will gravitate toward one or the other.

Self-Service vs. Concierge

Let's call the first type the *self-service* model. In this case, the cost of the product or service is so low that people are unwilling to pay much for customer support, e.g., not more than the price of the product itself. In this model, we will not only have to engineer the products or services so they're easy to use, but we must also make it easy for knowledgeable people to help each other when assistance is needed. In this case, support is mostly electronic and self-help related, with very little professional customer support human interaction required.

The second type of support is the *concierge* model, in which customers will pay a premium for lots of handholding and personalized, human-based customer support. Here, too, the majority of our efforts will be focused on ensuring customers don't have issues in the first place.

External Simplicity Masks Internal Complexity

With the explosion in the number of devices and technologies required to support those devices, I expect a fundamental shift in thinking in terms of support. The inherent economics require that very little support be provided. The narrow profit margins for many of these low-cost products mean extensive support could "break the bank" in terms of profitability.

But making something simple for customers means extra work for us. From a support viewpoint, external simplicity requires an increased amount of internal complexity. We will be forced to look at every possible reason a device fails, breaks or simply doesn't live up to the customer's expectations, then make sure that we develop a number of mitigating steps for each. None by itself will provide a foolproof solution, but taken together they should provide a lot of help.

Fuzzy Metrics

The future will bring a new vocabulary. New terms will help us understand and navigate the knowledge-based world we traverse. Most of today's support vocabulary is operations-based and is frankly meaningful only to those of us in the support world: calls abandoned, average speed of answer, etc. But increasingly, we are being asked what value we have contributed to the company.

Today, we don't have easy ways to measure this. We cannot comfortably articulate these kinds of activities. How many people *didn't* call us because they got the help they needed? How many issues did we avoid by ensuring a bug did not go out as originally scheduled? We can make estimates based on historical patterns, but we cannot say with any precision what *didn't* happen. We will get more comfortable with "fuzzy" metrics – metrics that cannot be precisely measured or reported on.

There are techniques that can give a sense of how a customer is doing. One example is Customer Lifetime Value. This is essentially a composite of different metrics, like first contact resolution rates, profitability, customer satisfaction scores, how long a customer has been a customer, how quickly they pay their bills etc. Metrics like these will become more popular as they will better showcase the value that support provides back to the company.

Application Hosting

Software companies will continue trying to move customers to an "on demand" service model, which is essentially a hosted model for software. In this scenario, customers pay a monthly fee to use software that resides on your company's servers, rather than the customers' hard drives.

With customers paying only for what they use, the concept is similar to a utility like water or electricity. You certainly don't need your own power plant to run a business. You may not even care what type of power source (coal, nuclear, hydro) your electricity comes from. All that's really important is that it's available and reliable. It's the same with application hosting.

This model will create a very different world for technology companies to operate in. Software will no longer be released once or twice a year. Sometimes it will be updated once or twice a month – even once or twice a day! There are far fewer tolerances for software bugs and less margin for error.

In this world, customers will wield a lot more influence. In effect, they are outsourcing all maintenance and upgrades to your support team. This is both good and bad. The good news is, you don't have to worry about a customer's infrastructures quite as much, or their implementation of your tools, or what version of your software they're running. It's all standardized, and you pretty much control it. The bad news is, you control it. Customers will be less tolerant of mistakes. Any mistakes that do slip through will ripple through the system quickly, and cause significant issues.

Listen and Learn

In the future, we will learn more and more from the rest of the world. Soon, future innovations will appear first in other parts of the world and then migrate here, rather than the other way around.

Scenario Planning

There is another more thoughtful technique for predicting the future: Scenario Planning. A number of books have focused on the subject, the definitive one perhaps being Peter Schwartz's *The Art of the Long View*.[6] There's only room for a brief examination of the topic in this chapter. To learn more, HDI offers its members a white paper titled "Scenario Planning: Preparing for an Uncertain Future" created by the HDI Strategic Advisory Board.[7]

Of course, even scenario planning does not guarantee that you'll be 100% right about the future. But it reduces the likelihood that you will be 100% wrong.

Lightning Quick Overview of Scenario Planning

The six basic steps of scenario planning are:

1. Identify the key question.
2. Research the facts related to the question.
3. Identify drivers that will influence the question.
4. Divide them into "certain" and "uncertain" drivers.
5. Develop four plausible scenarios about the future using uncertain drivers.
6. Develop scenario plots[8] that describe, in a dramatic manner, what life might be like in each of the scenarios.

After going through the scenario planning process, our team at HDI took an additional step. We looked at the implications of these scenarios for the future of technical support and customer service, some of which I'll share below.

Now let's go through these steps again in a bit more detail, as we attempt to catch a glimpse of the future of customer support.

Identify the Key Question

The key question we chose to examine was, "What will technical support be like in 10 years?"

Research the Facts Related to the Question

To help answer our question, we tapped into the collective experiences of the HDI Strategic Advisory Board, which HDI describes as "service and support industry's leading experts, Fortune 100 executives, media and analysts, vendor CEOs, and international representatives."

We spent a full day during our 2004 SAB meeting examining the *Future of Technical Support* paper. A smaller sub-group, comprised of Greg Oxton, Joe Fleischer and myself, followed up with numerous conference calls in which we debated the implications.

Identify Key Drivers that Influence the Key Question

We looked at drivers under the broad headings of *Society*, *Technology*, *Economic*, *Environmental* and *Politics*. We were not limited to these broad topics, of course, but they helped us focus and think outside our comfort zone of technology.

When identifying key drivers, the trick is to focus not just on the ones which are relatively easy to predict. As you'll see, the obvious ones are not particularly useful in forecasting the future.

One driver under the *Society* heading, for example, was the aging of the population. At first this seemed very obvious since, in general, life expectancy appears to be increasing all over the world.

But when we peeled back the onion and examined this statement a little more deeply, it turned out to be true only in certain places. There are dramatic regional variations. For example, about half of India's one billion people are under the age of 30. So its society is definitely not aging! In contrast, Italy's fertility rate is so low that its population is not only aging, it's actually dwindling.

Another driver influencing the future of technical support falls under the *Technology* category: the inexorable march of cheaper, faster computing. In affluent parts of the world, there may soon be hundreds of low-power, single-use computers per home, instead of the two or three PCs per home that we see today.

Once computers become so affordable that they reach the vast majority of humanity (including the segment that does not currently have any), the number of computing devices will multiply exponentially.

Under the *Environmental* heading, we examined the possibility of new laws being implemented to force companies to deal with the environmental impact of computer hardware disposal. As you know, this is already a serious environmental hazard. Every cathode ray tube (CRT) computer display and television picture tube contains approximately four to five pounds of lead, a toxic substance. In the United States alone, an estimated 1.2 billion pounds of lead could pollute soil and water sources if obsolete computers monitors and TVs are simply dumped in the trash, rather than disposed of properly.

Under *Politics,* the HDI team studied the rise of countries like China. We pondered, for example, what would happen if one day the Chinese government mandated that Mandarin Chinese would be the language of choice for technical support. Forget for a moment that Mandarin is too imprecise a language for this to be practical. What if the Chinese passed this law simply to flex its political muscle, not for practical reasons? What would be the implications for technical support?

Under the *Economic* category, we considered the possibility that new trading blocs might emerge and flex their economic muscle. What if these countries used their own interpretation of, say, intellectual property, rather than the predominantly western concept that exists today? In some cultures, for example, management ideas are the property of all humanity, not just those of who thought of them.

These are just a sample of the many drivers we considered and discussed at length. This is an important part of a scenario planning exercise. The more thought you put into it, the more value you get out of it. It's important for scenario planning groups to develop the ability to challenge each others' assumptions, and thus open up your understanding of the world.

Divide Drivers into "Certain" and "Uncertain" Categories

The next step in scenario planning involves dividing your list of drivers into two categories. A "certain" driver is one which you are reasonably confident will happen, even though you may not be sure exactly how it will play out. For example, we mentioned the aging population in certain parts of the world. That is a certain driver.

An "uncertain" driver, on the other hand, is one which we are not sure if or how it will ever actually happen. The possibility of powerful new trading blocs is a good example. With the rapid ascent of China as a manufacturing powerhouse, and of India as a software services powerhouse, what if these two countries formed an alliance of convenience into one massive trading bloc? If this ever happens, they would instantly become the largest trading bloc on earth, with almost 1.5 billion people. But of course, no one is certain it will ever happen.

What about terrorism and natural disasters like typhoons, cyclones and earthquakes? Should these be considered certain or uncertain? I consider them certain drivers. Obviously we don't know when or where they will happen, or how horrific the consequences will be, but we can state confidently that they will happen sooner or later.

Develop Four Plausible Future Scenarios Using Uncertain Drivers

After developing our long list of drivers, we separated the certain from the uncertain, and then set aside the certain drivers. It's not that they're useless, but for predicting the future using scenario planning, they have served their purpose.

Next, let's take our list of uncertain drivers. In one of the most difficult steps of the exercise, we'll select the two most influential attributes that most of the uncertain drivers fit into. Then we'll create two axes, resulting in four grids, each with a distinct and plausible scenario.

While it is certainly possible to come up with more than four scenarios, that number is easy to deal with and easy for people to wrap their minds around.

In our example, we felt that the two most influential attributes were *openness* and *personalization*. We mapped these attributes on the axis below.

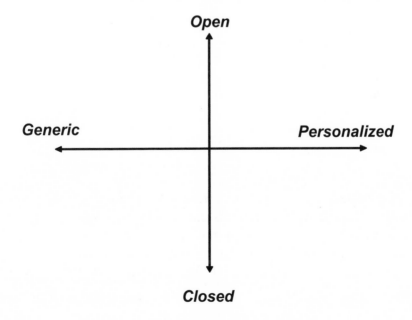

The openness axis represents a spectrum from open to closed; the personalization axis represents a spectrum from generic to personalized.

Next, we derive four quadrants from these two axes. Each quadrant, and the scenario associated with it, reflects different combinations of extremes of openness and personalization, as shown below.

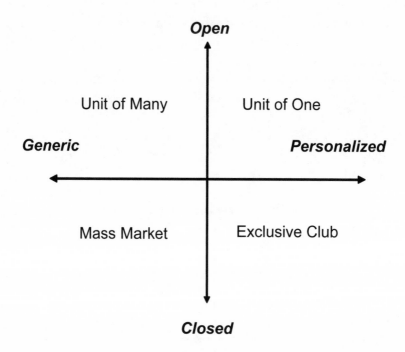

Let's dub these four scenarios *Unit of Many, Unit of One, Exclusive Club* and *Mass Market*, and take a closer look at each.

Remember, we are looking at these in the context of uncertain drivers under the general headings of *Society, Technology, Economic, Environmental* and *Politics*.

Unit of Many

Characteristics: Low degree of personalization, high degree of openness
In this scenario, the relationship is defined by who you are affiliated with. Among individuals who share the same affiliation, there's a greater willingness to help each other, but there is a lower degree of security and less adherence to rules.

Methods of communication develop which are not a barrier, and can transcend geographical boundaries and distance. In this scenario we anticipate real-time communication and simultaneous translation.

There is good flow of information. It is not hindered nor hoarded between different competing associations.

Since it is open, there are rich standards, leading to easy interoperability between different groups, whether they're political, economic, social or technical.

Unit of One

Characteristics: High degree of personalization, high degree of openness
In this scenario, relationships result from collaborations among individuals, rather than from interactions among groups. There is a high degree of personalization.

Individuals earn trust through specific, standardized achievements. In such a scenario, certification in different fields becomes a way to demonstrate mastery of a subject.

Members are most willing to communicate with others who share common interests and comparable status. The higher one's individual status, the greater one's access to others.

Exclusive Club

Characteristics: High degree of personalization, low degree of openness
Think of this as the "country club" model. In this scenario, getting access to the right group is very important, because it determines your status. Security is crucial, both to prevent gate

crashers as well as to safeguard those already inside. Security is a higher priority than communication between groups or clubs.

People must prove their trustworthiness by providing detailed, verifiable information about themselves before they can earn permission to interact with others.

The prime advantage in this scenario isn't affiliation or status; it's access to other trustworthy individuals.

Mass Market

Characteristics: Low degree of personalization, low degree of openness
The prime commodity in this scenario isn't affiliation with smaller groups, status or access to others. It's the customer record.

Within the larger blocs, rules are far-reaching, and determine the manner in which individuals can communicate and collaborate.

Service and support, not to mention communication in general, are defined by legal, linguistic and technological boundaries that are erected by different groups or blocs.

Plot the Future in Each Scenario

If you do the scenario planning exercise well, each of the four quadrants should be equally plausible. There should be no favorites among them. Since this exercise is all about the future, the best way to make the abstract seem real is to illustrate what the future might be like in each of the scenarios, using slightly exaggerated stories. Develop plots that illustrate, in a dramatic manner, what the future might be like in each of the scenarios.

Imagine Service and Support in Each Scenario

Let's go through each of our scenarios and see what the implications for technical support may be.

Unit of Many *(Generic and Open)*

In this scenario, while there are multiple technical standards, there is good interoperability between them.

Demand for support among end users is low. A lot of generic information is available in the public domain, but not much proprietary or secret information.

Furthermore, because of all the information available, end users are unwilling to pay for support. Instead, they support each other (community model).

Because of rich standards and a high level of interoperability, there will be far more sophisticated self-healing and self-monitoring done.

Because people will not pay for support, some will opt to move to a different system if they need a lot of support. Thus, most support will have to be at the infrastructure level and be transparent to end users.

In order for this to happen, there will be high internal complexity (for those who provide support) and low external complexity (for those who receive support).

Unit of One *(Personalized and Open)*

Although demand for support is high among these end users, they're unwilling to pay for it unless it's bundled with other high-value offerings.

Because it is personalized, support is highly customized. Yet it is globally applicable due to the openness between blocs.

Since there are standards, support is highly automated, which reduces external complexity for the end user. Where end users do encounter complexity is the degree to which they can customize the support they receive.

Exclusive Club *(Personalized and Closed)*

Demand for support among end users is quite high, and users are willing to pay a lot for highly personalized support.

Support is highly customized, based on the customer's location and the applications he or she is using.

Those who provide support will require skills to assist users with proprietary systems and applications that may not interoperate with one another.

Support is often on-site and in person, rather than anonymously over a network.

For the sake of security, support employs minimal automation; it is a labor-intensive process.

External complexity drives the demand for rich support capabilities.

Mass Market (Generic and Closed)

Users' support requirements reflect their locations and the devices they use. Support is specific to products and tailored to the enterprise.

Support is available through contracts, which offer many choices of service levels.

Demand for support is moderate, but end users are generally unwilling to pay for support. Nevertheless, if end users don't have contracts, they are on their own.

The account represents the primary relationship between those who provide support and those who receive it, so it's crucial for support organizations to maintain ownership of their accounts.

Support reps require a broad range of skills to support proprietary systems and applications that don't necessarily work with one another.

12 Final Thoughts

Expecting the world to treat you fairly because you are a good person is a little like expecting the bull not to attack you because you are a vegetarian.

– *Dennis Wholey, television commentator*

An increasing number of companies around the world provide good customer support.[1] They are quick to respond to issues, and quick to resolve each issue to the customer's satisfaction. As we have discussed throughout the book, unfortunately, that's not enough. Taking really good care of customers after they have an issue only shows that you provide good service, not great service.

Delivering great service means making sure customers don't have issues in the first place. To move up to delivering "great" service requires a profound mindset change. This means optimizing people, process and technology to look at things from a customer perspective so that the cost, delays and frustrations with a customer having an issue with your product or service are minimized since issues are eliminated in the first place.

The customer support profession is at a crossroads, which places customer support executives at a critical juncture in our corporate careers. We can either break through and step up as senior executives in our organization and unleash the power of the customer throughout our organization, or continue to play a vital but short-lived role taking care of customer complaints.

I'm confident that we have the skills and confidence to take our place as senior executives in the company. This book is merely a reflection of some of what I've learned from others on my still-unfinished journey to becoming an Ultimate Customer Support Executive.

As you make your own journey on this path, please be sure to give back to the community by sharing your experiences with others. I'd love to hear your comments and experiences. Please do get in touch with me. You can find my contact information at my website: www.verghisgroup.com.

Appendix:
Standards

Standards: ISO 9000

When it comes to quality standards, the ISO 9000 Series[1] is perhaps the best known in the world.

Issued by the International Standards Organization in Geneva, Switzerland, ISO 9000 Series standards and guidelines focus on continual improvement of customer satisfaction through the use of an effective and efficient business management system. The ultimate intent of ISO 9000 is to assist companies best serve their customers.

ISO 9000 is essentially about improving management processes. It seeks to ensure that processes are defined and followed, and requires evidence that they are.

There are three standards that make up the ISO 9000 Series:

- ISO 9001, for companies with the capability to design goods and services
- ISO 9002, for companies that provide (but do not design) goods & services, and
- ISO 9003, which focuses on the final inspection and test processes within an organization

For customer service organizations, I don't think ISO 9000 is robust enough. Still, it's useful to know about. In many countries, ISO 9000 is seen as an important indicator of quality, and is sometimes a requirement in RFPs (Requests for Proposals) from a sourcing company.

Capability Maturity Model Integration

If you deal with software development you probably have heard of CMM[2] (Capability Maturity Model).

While not strictly an IT service or support model, CMM was created to improve the software development process. CMM guides development along an evolutionary path from chaotic, *ad hoc* processes to mature, disciplined development systems.

CMM, developed by Carnegie Mellon's Software Engineering Institute, describes the principles and practices underlying software development process maturity. CMM has since been absorbed by CMMI –Capability Maturity Model Integration – which added a level zero (Not Performed) to CMM's famed five level model:

- Level 1: Performed Informally
- Level 2: Planned and Tracked
- Level 3: Well-Defined
- Level 4: Quantitatively Controlled
- Level 5: Continuously Improving

Several of the largest outsourcing outfits in India have achieved the highest level of CMMI certification – Level 5. They take CMMI seriously and use it as a competitive differentiator to help them win lucrative software outsourcing contracts. While other parts of the world also boast CMMI Level 5 organizations, the majority are based in India.

More recently, the CMMI model has been expanded to include maturity models for People, Software Acquisition, Systems Engineering, Integrated Product Development and IT Services.

The reason you should be aware of CMMI is because a large number of outsourcers are CMMI certified. If you are considering outsourcing all or part of your support, this is something that is worth getting familiar with, to help you work better with the outsourcing partner.

Note: Here's one difference between ISO 9001 and CMMI. ISO 9001 specifies only a minimal acceptable quality level for software processes, while CMMI establishes a framework for continuous process improvement. CMMI is also more explicit than ISO in defining the means to achieving that end.

IT Services Qualification Center

Another initiative from Carnegie Mellon University, the IT Services Qualification Center[3] (ITsqc) works on ways to improve IT outsourcing relationships. ITsqc created the Qualification Center model for three reasons:

1. To help IT-enabled sourcing service providers appraise and improve their ability to provide high quality sourcing services
2. To provide a way for providers to differentiate themselves from the competition
3. To help prospective clients evaluate service providers

ITsqc has begun a related effort to model best practices of IT-enabled sourcing clients. The goal of the eSourcing Capability Model for Clients is to assist client organizations continuously evolve, improve, and innovate their capabilities, so they can develop stronger, longer, and more trusting relationships with their service providers.

BS 15000

BS 15000[4] is another formal standard, developed jointly by BSI (UK's National Standards Body), OGC (owners of ITIL) and itSMF (the IT Service Management Forum).

Based on ITIL, BS 15000 covers all the ITIL processes, and was written to co-exist with the current version of ITIL publications.

BS 15000 defines requirements covering ITIL Service Support & Delivery and Security Management and Relationship

Management that must be satisfied to be labeled a quality ITSM solution. It also contains generic Quality Management clauses that align it with ISO 9001 and ITIL.

BS 15000 certification is managed by the itSMF.

CoBIT and BS 7799 (ISO 17799)

COBIT[5] (Control Objectives for Information and related Technology) and ISO 17799 are standards focusing on security. Both are probably well known by the security and risk management teams in your organization.

Issued by the IT Governance Institute, COBIT is now in its third edition. It is increasingly accepted internationally as a good set of practices for control over information, IT and related risks. It uses a maturity model as a means of assessing the maturity of a company's processes and to help organizations set their maturity goals for these processes.

The maturity levels are:

- Non-existent
- Initial/Ad-hoc
- Repeatable but Intuitive
- Defined Process
- Managed and Measurable
- Optimized

BS 7799 is an IT security standard, perhaps the most widely recognized in the world. What began as simply a British standard has evolved into an international standard called ISO 17799.

ISO 17799[6] focuses on security, not processes. It is a comprehensive approach to IT security, and complying with it requires meeting stringent standards.

Organizations can create ITIL processes, then use ISO 17799 to prove that their information is secure and protected at all times.

Endnotes

Chapter 1

1. An "elevator speech" is so called because it refers to the short amount of time you have to get someone's attention – about the time you are together in an elevator (or lift).

Chapter 2

1. IT Infrastructure Library. You will read more about it in Chapter 5, *Process*.
2. "Rookie" is another term for beginner. If you are a computer gamer, the term is "noob," a derogative form of "newbie."

Chapter 3

1. If you don't have the list of all customers handy, finance or sales will be able to get one for you. Don't forget to include customers that come through your reseller and international channels.
2. The specific term is DSO – "Days Sales Outstanding." More about DSOs in Chapter 11, *Being Recognized*.
3. "Want to Perfect Your Company's Service? Use Behavioral Science," *Harvard Business Review,* June, 2001
4. "Information, Choice and Reactions to Stress: A Field Experiment in a Blood Bank with Laboratory Analogue," R.T. Mills and D.S. Krantz, *Journal of Personality and Social Psychology,* 1979
5. www.wjh.harvard.edu/~na/surgeons%20tone%20of%20voice.pdf
6. harvardbusinessonline.hbsp.harvard.edu/b01/en/common/item_detail.jhtml?id=F0205A
7. Principal of Great Brook Consulting (www.greatbrook.com), author of *Customer Surveying: A Guidebook for Service Managers,* Frederick C. Van Bennekom (Customer Service Press)
8. www.verghisgroup.com

Chapter 4

1. They are certainly in the minority. "World class" customer support is in a pretty sorry state.

Chapter 5

1. For the purposes of this example, let's assume you only get incoming queries via the phone.
2. This made sense because Akamai's customers were second level support staff from companies like Yahoo, Microsoft, Apple and CNN.
3. *Hotel Secrets from the Travel Detective*, Peter Greenberg (Random House)
4. When people do thank you, they can do it in rather memorable ways. While at Duke University's Office of Information Technology, the Help Desk team got champagne and cookies as a thank you from a professor who thought we had gone out of our way to help! This had a profound impact on the team's morale and often outstanding service was lauded internally as a "champagne-worthy" event.
5. The Consulting Psychologists Press Inc. administers the Myers-Briggs tests.
6. www.cio.com/leadership/edit/la101504_better.html
7. *Career Anchors: Discovering Your Real Values,* Edgar H. Schein (Pfeiffer)
8. Obviously you would engage Human Resources very early on in the process, and follow their guidance.
9. Check with your Human Resources department first. Some cautious companies prohibit employers from giving any sort of reference post layoff for fear of lawsuits.
10. www.nwfusion.com/news/1997/1229duke.html
11. The real old timers among us may recall one typically hidden-from-customer term: RTFM (Read The [Expletive] Manual.) When was the last time you read a manual before starting a new application?
12. www.thinkhdi.com and follow links to *Individual Certification*
13. www.thesspa.com

14. www.stiknowledge.com
15. www.verghisgroup.com
16. www.copc.com
17. www.thinkhdi.com (Disclaimer: In the interests of full disclosure, I am a certified auditor for the HDI's Support Center Certification.)
18. www.servicestrategies.com
19. www.stiknowledge.com

Chapter 6

1. www.thegateway.org/help/about/documentation/gem-controlled-vocabularies/vocabulary-resource-type
2. www.ogc.gov.uk
3. www.ogc.gov.uk
4. www.itsmf.com
5. An additional business perspective book is due to be published in the first half of 2005. *Business Perspective Volume 2* looks at IT delivery from a business viewpoint.
6. www.iseb.org.uk
7. www.exin-exams.com
8. www.thinkhdi.com
9. www.motorola.com/motorolauniversity
10. www.serviceinnovation.org
11. www.bscol.com

Chapter 7

1. I have maintained the Phil Verghis' Help Desk FAQ on a volunteer basis since 1993. You can find it at: www.verghisgroup.com/resources.html
2. *Dabba* means *box* in Hindi, the national language of India. So *dabbawallah* literally means *box person.*

Chapter 8

1. www.geert-hofstede.com
2. Stanford University Press
3. www.lisa.org

Chapter 9

1. This chapter draws heavily on work done by the HDI Strategic Advisory Board in 2004, when I was chair of the HDI SAB. A white paper is available to HDI members at www.thinkhdi.com.
2. These definitions are from HDI's Strategic Advisory Board.
3. The FCC defines high-speed Internet connections as those exceeding 200 Kbps.
4. *Living on the Fault Line: Managing for Shareholder Value in the Age of the Internet,* Geoffrey Moore (HarperBusiness; May, 2000)

Chapter 10

1. In many countries you are required by law to inform the customer that the call is being monitored or recorded.
2. I'm intentionally excluding customer surveys, which should already be part of your day-to-day operations.
3. Other groups like STI Knowledge (www.stiknowledge.com) and COPC (www.copc.com) offer more call center-like certifications. I'm focusing on customer support (both internal and external) that is more technically oriented.
4. Disclaimer: I am a certified SCC auditor.
5. www.servicestrategies.com
6. www.asponline.com
7. www.thesspa.com

Chapter 11

1. www.wimaxforum.org
2. www.zigbee.org
3. www.bluetooth.com
4. www.wi-fi.org
5. news.bbc.co.uk/2/hi/business/1386310.stm
6. *The Art of the Long View: Planning for the Future in an Uncertain World,* Peter Schwartz (Currency)
7. www.thinkhdi.com
8. For an HDI white paper titled *The Future of Technical Support – 10 Years Out,* go to www.thinkhdi.com and follow links to the white papers section.

Appendix: Standards

1. www.iso.org
2. www.sei.cmu.edu/cmm/cmm.html
3. itsqc.cs.cmu.edu
4. www.bs15000certification.com
5. www.isaca.org/cobit.htm
6. www.iso17799.net

Index